YOU CAN TEACH YOURSELF

FINGERPICKING GUITAR

by Tommy Flint

CD CONTENTS*

1	Tuning the Guitar [2:29]	
2	The First Chords [:44]	
3	The First Chords with Drums [:24]	
4	The First Picking Pattern (slow & fast) [:48]	
5	Four String Chords (slow & fast) [1:03]	
6	Arpeggio (slow & fast) [1:02]	
7	Five & Six String Chords (C & G7, slow & fast) [1:02]	
8	Skip to My Lou (rhythm) [:27]	
9	Skip to My Lou (rhythm & melody) [:39]	
10	A Chord Study (E, A, & B7)- Walking Blues [1:17]	
11	A New Picking Pattern [:25]	
12	Playing Between the Beats [:30]	
13	A Chord Progression Used for Many Songs (4/4) [:33]	
14	A Chord Progression Used for Many Songs (3/4) [:27]	
15	Accompaniment [:22]	

16	Accompaniment & Melody (3 & 1) [1:05]
17	Lonesome Polecat [:38]
18	Hitting on All Four [:27]
19	The Second Time (slow & fast) [:45]
20	In the Early Morning Mist [:57]
21	On the Appalachian Trail [:38]
22	The Bluestem Slopes [:46]
23	Stepping Out (slow & fast) [1:07]
24	Little Brown Jug (slow) [:46]
25	Little Brown Jug (fast) [:37]
26	The Fiery Skipper [:33]
27	Luna's Tune (slow) [:56]
28	Luna's Tune (fast) [:42]
29	He's Got the Whole World in His Hands (slow) [:45]
30	He's Got the Whole World in His Hands (fast) [:57]
31	Snap Crackle, Crackle and Bang [:46]
32	Albert Lea Ann [1:21]
33	Riding Out of Dodge [1:01]

34	Key of C Alternative Bass Notes [:28]
35	Key of G Alternative Bass Notes [:24]
36	Key of D Alternative Bass Notes [:20]
37	Key of A Alternative Bass Notes [:20]
38	Key of E Alternative Bass Notes [:16]
39	Key of Am Alternative Bass Notes [:19]
40	Key of Em Alternative Bass Notes [:22]
41	Key of Dm Alternative Bass Notes [:17]
42	Key of Fm Alternative Bass Notes [:20]
43	Lonely Guitar [:51]
44	Bury Me Beneath the Willow (slow) [:37]
45	Bury Me Beneath the Willow (fast) [:30]
46	A Triplet Study- House of the Rising Sun [:30]
47	With Melody- House of the Rising Sun [1:07]
48	A Minor Study [:36]
49	Syncopation [2:06]
50	Blue River Train (slow) [1:08]
51	Blue River Train (fast) [:43]

52	Powder House Blues [1:17]
53	Quaker Notes [:41]
54	Legend of the Carpathians [1:08]
55	The Carnival of Venice (slow) [:38]
56	The Carnival of Venice (fast) [:29]
57	Wildwood Flower (slow) [:42]
58	Wildwood Flower (fast) [:33]
59	How to Play in Any Key [2:21]
60	Stomping on the Steppe [1:06]
61	Satisfaction Guaranteed (slow) [:36]
62	Satisfaction Guaranteed (fast) [:32]
63	Etude [1:00]
64	Amazing Grace [:48]
65	The Ballad of Jesse James [:56]
66	Cockles and Mussels [:32]
67	Some Very Useful Patterns [1:27]
68	Aura Lee [1:04]
69	The Rolling Flint Hills [:51]
70	Once Upon a Time [:57]
71	Genoa Holiday [:46]

*This book is available as a book only or as a book/compact disc configuration.

If you have purchased the book only, recordings (96498C), (96498CD) of the music in this book is now available. The publisher strongly recommends the use of this resource along with the text to insure accuracy of interpretation and ease in learning.

MEL BAY®

1 2 3 4 5 6 7 8 9 0

Visit us on the Web at www.melbay.com — E-mail us at email@melbay.com

CONTENTS

"The city of Drakesboro named a westside street Tommy Flint Avenue....
It joins other streets named for [Mose] Rager, [Merle] Travis, John Prine
and other musical notables.
'When I was a bashful kid coming down here to Mose Rager's barber
shop, I didn't have any idea my name would be on anything,' said Flint....
'It's really great. It's an honor.'"

Taken from an article by Greg Kocher, Messenger-Inquirer

DEDICATION

*To my children Tom, Robin, Tammy,
Terry, Travis, Kelly, and Patrick
and their loved ones.*

PREFACE

The purpose of this book and companion video, or recording, is to teach and help you to play the guitar in the shortest possible time. I believe you will learn enough in the first lesson that you will enjoy playing it on your guitar. But remember, the more the guitar is in your hands the faster you will learn. Like most things, the more you do it the easier it becomes, and the more technical ability you acquire. But it needs to be fun, something enjoyable. These lessons are enjoyable while at the same time very informative and great technique builders.

Learning more about the guitar and how to grow as a musician and become a better guitarist is a never ending process. The more you play the more you learn, and the more you learn, the more things you are capable of playing.

I prefer the word play rather than practice. To practice the guitar is nothing more than to play the instrument, but play sounds pleasant, while to many people practice connotes work. At the beginning I feel that it is good to play melodies and learn tunes you like. As you grow and become a better musician, I believe you will also grow to enjoy playing scales and exercises because you will see how beneficial they are.

After all these years I think I never pick up my guitar that I don't learn something or, something I had been wondering about suddenly becomes clear to me. Also, just holding the guitar and absentmindedly playing chords or runs I sometimes happen to come up with a new melody.

I had no formal lessons. I learned some open string chords from my mother. I began leaning to read music from a book my parents ordered from the Montgomery Ward catalog. We didn't have videos or tape recorders in those days, so I listened to the radio and tried to remember what I heard long enough to find something similar on my guitar. I watched guitar players and memorized how their fingers were located on the strings and frets, and learned chords that way.

I heard Merle Travis on the radio and tried to duplicate his sound and soon met Mose Rager who Travis learned from. I "haunted" his barbershop, begging him to play, and memorized his chords and the tunes he played. Soon I met Chet Atkins who one day introduced me to Merle Travis. These three men Travis, Atkins and Rager were my boyhood heroes. I taught myself to read music by studying method books. I learned theory, harmony, chord construction etc. from books and questioning musicians whom I respected.

I gained invaluable on the job experience playing all types of shows, some of which required reading and some which were strictly improvised, where I never met the featured performer until he/she walked on stage. I have been very fortunate in being able to work with and learn from great musicians. I have also worked with some less than great, but, I have never played a job on which I did not learn. Sometimes I learned what not to do.

Over the years I have learned from many sources. I have recordings by jazz, classical and country guitarists as well as pianists, sax and trumpet players, dixieland, bebop, modern jazz, blues, big band, etc. There is no end. So let's begin with lesson one and enjoy.

WARNING

If you are not absolutely certain that you want to become a guitar player, do not buy this book. Playing the guitar may be addictive. Recovery from playing the guitar is very difficult, if not impossible. In most cases it's "once a guitar player, always a guitar player."

Symptoms are: Recurring or sometimes constant thoughts about guitars. Always longing to hold a guitar, to feel its smooth, graceful neck and gently stroke its delicate strings, to learn more and more chords, more songs, new and different methods of plucking and strumming the strings. The pure joy of playing beautiful music.

BEWARE: If you display one or more of these symptoms you may be BECOMING A GUITARIST!

YOU DO NOT HAVE TO READ MUSIC TO USE THIS BOOK

Reading music is not a requirement for using this book. The lessons presented here utilize tablature, which is an extremely fast and easy method to use for learning lessons and arrangements in this book and most books written specifically for guitar.

I use tab with all my beginning students because, I feel it is very important that the beginner learns to play some melodies or songs as soon as possible, even in the first lesson. When he/she has learned how to play songs, change chords, keep time, has developed some finger dexterity and has some knowledge of the fingerboard and is actually a guitar player, then, learning standard music notation is a rewarding experience, is pleasurable and a more accelerated process.

Near the end of this book you will find a few more short paragraphs on tablature. When you have completed this book or, when you feel that you are ready or would like to begin learning standard music notation, I would recommend my book "DELUXE FINGERSTYLE GUITAR METHOD" Volume I, Mel Bay Publications, #4 Industrial Drive, Pacific, MO. 63069-0066.

THE GUITAR PARTS

(REFER TO THIS CHART OFTEN)

ACOUSTIC GUITAR

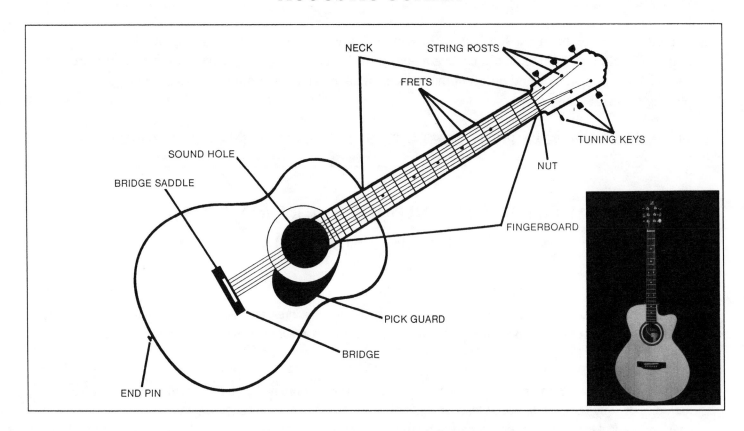

ELECTRIC GUITAR

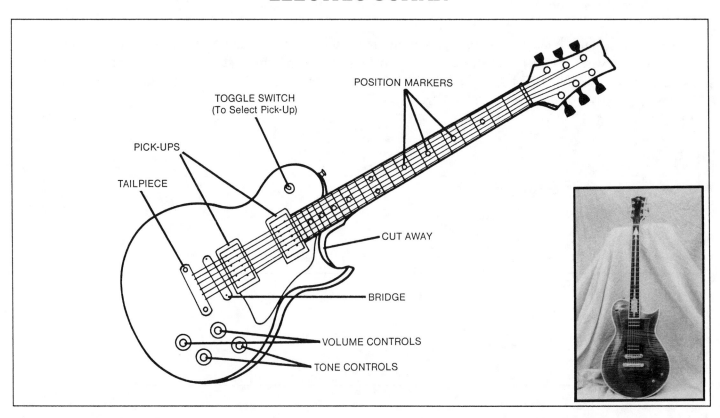

HOW TO SELECT A GUITAR

Most any type of guitar can be used for playing fingerstyle, nylon string acoustic or classical, nylon string electric, steel string acoustic or acoustic/electric, hollow body or semi hollow body electric or, solid body electric. Each type of guitar has a different feel.

Nylon strings are soft and easy on the fingers if, they are fairly close to the fingerboard. They are very good for the beginner. However, light gauge steel strings are excellent for the beginner.

It is very important that the guitar is easy to play and that it tunes true, i.e. the strings are close to the fingerboard and easy to press against the frets and they are in tune over the entire fingerboard. Also the neck needs to be straight and free of warp or bow. Most good steel string guitars have an adjustable steel rod (truss rod) in the neck which can be used to straighten the neck in case it does develop a bow.

If you are a beginner, I would suggest you purchase the guitar from a reputable dealer or have an experienced guitarist try it out, play it, check the action and tuning, and, if it is electric, make sure all the controls are working.

You will need a case to protect your guitar, probably a chipboard case if you begin learning on an inexpensive model. A hard-shell case is a must when you purchase your nice guitar. Also, don't leave your guitar near extreme heat or cold, even if it is in the case. Leaving it in the trunk of your car on very hot summer days or very cold winter days is extremely risky. It can cause cracks or checks in the finish and has even been known to crack the wood.

HOW TO HOLD THE GUITAR

SOME SITTING POSITIONS

In the above positions the guitar rests on the right leg and is held against the body by the right forearm.

For this position the right leg is elevated by use of a footstool.

STANDING

In the standing position, the guitar is supported by a strap over the shoulder, as shown above.

Standing or sitting on a high stool is preferred by many professionals. That way you are in full view of the entire audience. It is also easier to get to the microphone and move around the stage to keep the audience's attention.

SITTING ON A HIGH STOOL

THE CLASSICAL POSITION

For the classical style the guitar is held on the left leg, which is elevated by placing the foot on a stool. The guitar is held against the body by the left forearm. Both hands need to be free and should not be used to support the weight of the instrument. The neck should be at approximately a forty-five degree angle. Sit erect and hold the guitar in a vertical position. Don't allow it to lean at an angle from front to back.

TUNING THE GUITAR

I would advise using an electronic tuner for now, while your ears are developing and your tuning skills are being refined. The tuner will show you visually when the guitar is in tune. You can purchase a tuner at most any music store. If you don't have a tuner, ask a friend who plays to tune it or, I think an instructor at a music store or school would be happy to tune it for you the first time, or two. It will take some time, patience and experimentation, but tuning will soon be easy for you. There are various methods of tuning such as : by octaves, harmonics, chord inversions etc. The three three most common methods are shown below.

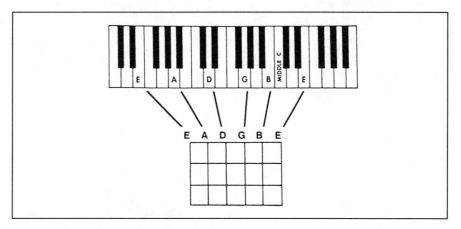

The six open strings of the guitar are the same pitch as the six notes shown on the piano keyboard. The first string is above middle C. The other five strings are below middle C.

If the piano and pitch pipe are unavailable:

1. Tighten the 6th sting until you get a good clear tone.
2. Place the finger on the 6th string behind the 5th fret. This will give you the pitch of the open ⑤ th string.
3. Place the finger on the 5th string behind the 5th fret to get the pitch of the open 4th sting.
4. Place the finger on the 4th string behind the 5th fret to get the pitch of the open 3rd string.
5. Place the finger on the 3rd string behind the 4th fret to get the pitch of the open 2nd string.
6. Place the finger on the 2nd string behind the 5th fret to obtain the tone of the open 1st string.

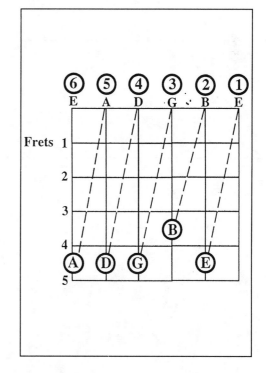

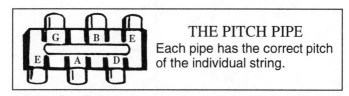

THE PITCH PIPE
Each pipe has the correct pitch of the individual string.

The tones of the strings are at the beginning of the recording so we will be tuned together. If you have an electric tuner, you will most likely be in tune with the recording.

RIGHT-HAND NOTATION

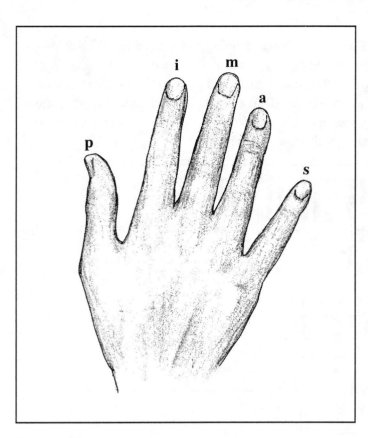

Fingers of the right hand will be indicated by the letters:

p - THUMB or PULGAR

i - INDEX or INDICE

m - MIDDLE or MEDIO

a - RING FINGER or ANULAR

s - LITTLE FINGER

The letters indicating the fingers will appear above, below or to the right of the notes in musical notation and/or the numbers in tablature.

LEFT-HAND NOTATION

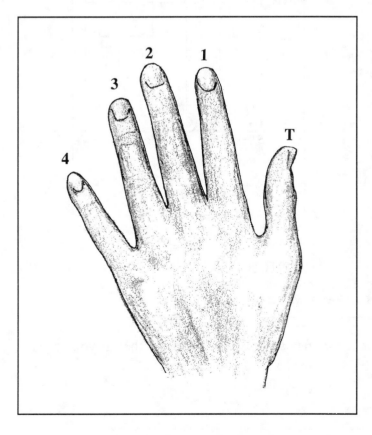

The fingers of the left hand will be indicated by numbers. The thumb will be indicated by the letter "T." The numbers will appear in chord diagrams and above, below or to the left of the notes in musical notation.

THE THUMB PICK

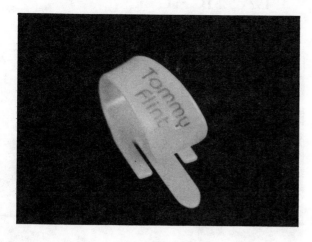 

The thumb pick is optional. Classical guitarists don't use picks. However, I prefer using the thumb pick, especially when playing on steel or bronze strings. It is needed for Travis Picking in order to get the drive and authority, and it's very useful for blues and ragtime. The thumb pick can be used for alternate picking (down and up strokes) fiddle tunes, hoe-downs, jazz licks, etc. I use medium weight picks most of the time. I sometimes use a heavy pick when playing on heavy gauge strings, or to get more punch. The pick fits as shown in the photo below. It should fit firmly so it won't turn or slide off, but it also needs to feel comfortably. Experiment with different sizes and shapes until you find the pick that is right for you.

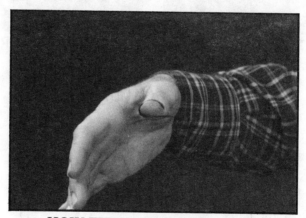

HOW THE THUMB PICK FITS

THE RIGHT HAND POSITION FOR STYLES OTHER THAN CLASSICAL

Let the hand hang in a relaxed position over the strings. Now place the thumb on either the fifth or sixth string, the index finger on the third string, middle finger on the second string, and the third finger on the first string. Now your hand is in the proper playing position. This may vary with different styles, but basically this is the correct position.

Remember to relax.

The wrist should remain stationary at all times when playing fingerstyle. Use the fingers only. Just curl them in toward the palm of the hand as if making a loose fist.

BEFORE PLUCKING THE STRINGS

AFTER PLUCKING

FINGERNAILS

RIGHT HAND

The nails should be filed to the approximate shape or contour of the fingers' tips. They should extend slightly past the finger tips approximately 1/16 inch. It is advisable to carry an emery board to keep the nails smooth and in playing condition.

Grade 600 sandpaper may be used to smooth the nails.

Generally speaking, it is not wise to play heavy steel or bronze strings with the bare fingers. You may wear the nail down and cause gaps and notches to appear in them.

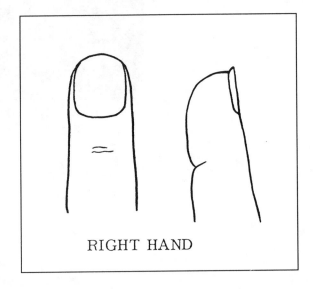

RIGHT HAND

THE LEFT HAND

The nails of the left hand should be filed very short so as not to interfere with holding down the strings and making chords. They should also be very smooth so they won't hang up on the strings and cause sloppy technique.

THE LEFT HAND POSITION

Place the fingers firmly on the strings very close to the frets. Bend the fingers and use the finger tips, unless you are holding down more than one string with the same finger. Then the finger should lay flat on the fingerboard. Generally, the ball or pad (never the tip) of the thumb should remain on the back of the guitar neck. Do not bend the thumb. Occasionally it may be necessary to use the thumb on the bass strings on some chords. In this case it will obviously be essential that you bend the thumb.

If the strings buzz or rattle, slide the fingers up closer to the frets. Remember to keep the fingers arched so they will not touch other strings and deaden them.

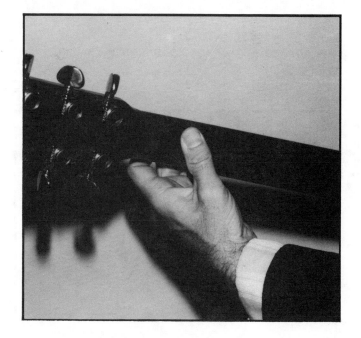

The correct position of the thumb
Classical position
Also used for single string picking

Position of the left hand when using
the thumb on the bass strings

The correct position of the thumb
Back View

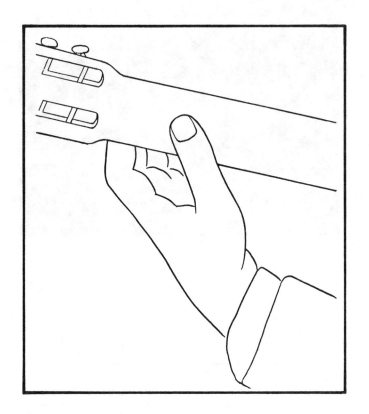

The correct position of the thumb
Side View

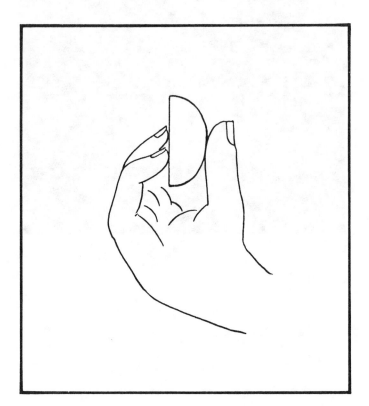

THE FINGERBOARD
CHORD DIAGRAMS

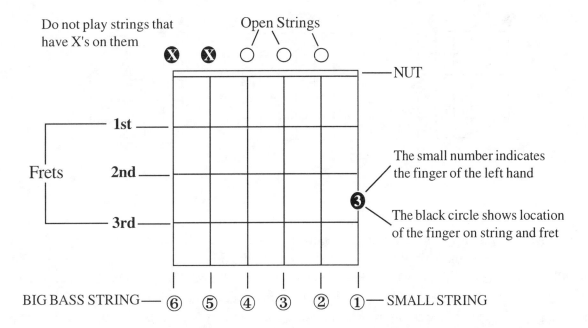

Do not play strings that have X's on them

Open Strings

NUT

Frets

1st

2nd

3rd

The small number indicates the finger of the left hand

3

The black circle shows location of the finger on string and fret

BIG BASS STRING — ⑥ ⑤ ④ ③ ② ① — SMALL STRING

The vertical lines are the strings. The horizontal lines are the frets. The encircled numerals are the string numbers. Open string = Do not touch string with the left hand. <u>Do</u> pick string with the right hand.

HOW TO FINGER CHORDS

When making a chord, the fingers should be arched so the finger tips are pressing the strings straight in toward the fingerboard. Care should be taken that no finger touches a string other than the one it is depressing. The fingers should be placed firmly on the strings, as close to the frets as possible without getting directly on them.

THE FIRST CHORDS

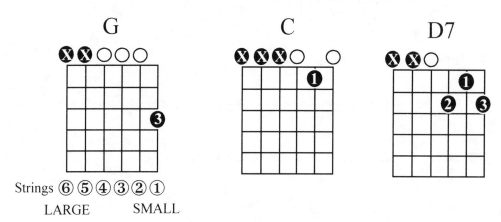

Okay, let's play the first three chords. Place your third finger on the ① st string very close to the third fret as shown in the diagram. Press the string against the fret just firm enough to get a clear tone. If the note sounds dead or muffled press more firmly. If you get a buzz move the finger closer to the fret. Use the fingertip and press inward toward the fingerboard. Now, using the thumb of the right hand, move it downward strumming the ③ rd, ② nd and ① st strings. Make sure the finger is not touching the open ② nd string. Keep adjusting the finger until the strings ring clear. Now you are ready to play the C chord. Place the tip of your first finger on the ② nd string, first fret. Make sure it doesn't touch the open ① st or ③ rd string. Experiment until the chord sounds clear.

Repeat this procedure with D7 chord. It will seem difficult at first, but be persistant and keep experimenting and in a short while it will be a very easy chord for you. When changing from D7 to G simply lift the first and second fingers and slide the third finger to the third fret.

Next, play the chords in tempo. Slowly count one, two, three, four, and space the counts as evenly as the ticks of a clock. Strum G chord on the first four counts, C chord on the next four, then D7 on the next four and go back to G for the last four. Play the chords until you can keep a steady rhythm without pausing between chords. The strums are indicated by diagonal lines. The vertical lines are called bars. The space between two bars is a measure. Songs are divided into measures by bars.

A THUMB STRUM

Use the thumb only to strum the ③ rd, ② nd and ① st strings.

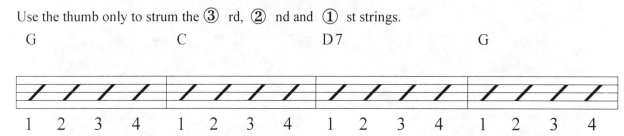

Very good! Now you are ready to learn a picking pattern. Allow the fingers of your right hand to hang loosely over the strings. Now place your thumb (p) on the ③rd string, the index finger (i) on the ②nd string and the middle finger (m) on the ①st string. Move the p downward picking the ③rd string. Then curl the (i) finger in toward the palm and pick the ②nd string. Next curl the m finger in and pick the ①st, then go back and pick the ②nd string with (i) finger. Repeat this pattern several times while counting 1 2 3 4 and picking one string on each count. SPACE THE COUNTS EVENLY!

THE FIRST PICKING PATTERN

1   2   3   4   SIMILE

Congratulations! You have just played your first fingerstyle pattern.

ADDING A FINGER TO C CHORD, AND TWO NEW CHORDS

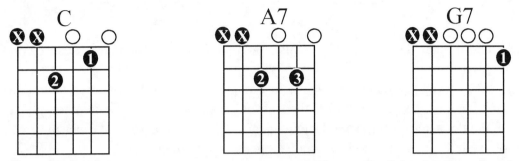

When you play a chord you are playing three or more notes. The tones of the chord can be played simultaneously, as when you use the thumb to strum the strings all together, or as near together as possible. Or the tones can be played separately or in succession, as when you pluck a different string with each finger and thumb. The term for this is "arpeggio."

THUMB STRUM

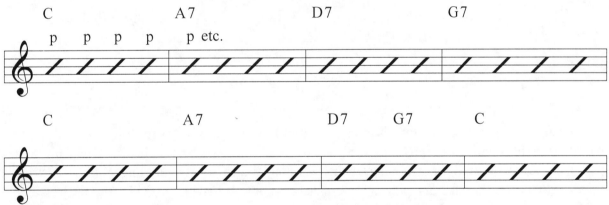

In the following arpeggiated chord progression use the thumb (p) on the ④ th string, i finger on the ③ rd, m on the the ② nd and a on the ① st.

ARPEGGIO

FIVE AND SIX STRING CHORDS

C

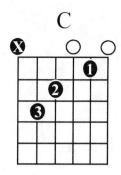

G7

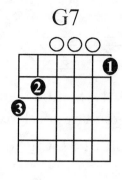

Now, make C chord, then place your right thumb (p) on the ⑤ string, the index finger (i) on the ③ string, middle finger (m) on the ② string and ring finger (a) on the ① string. Without removing your thumb from the ⑤ string, just make believe the fingers are glued together and curl them in toward the palm as if making a loose fist and pluck the three strings at the same time. Remember, play the strings all together so the three strings will sound simultaneously. Repeat this several times until you can do it and remain relaxed. Remember the fingers move together as if glued.

You are now ready to play the following chord progression. Play the bass string on the first and third beats, then pluck the treble strings on the second and fourth beats. The encircled numbers above the bass notes indicate the string to play with your thumb.

PLAYING RHYTHM GUITAR

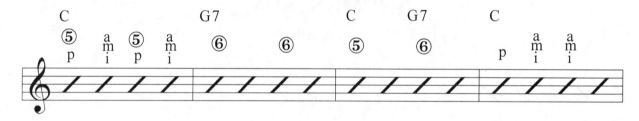

Hearing the same bass note over and over is monotonous and soon becomes very tiresome. To add variety we can play alternate bass notes. Make a C chord, then play the ⑤ string on the first beat and then pluck the treble strings as usual. Now, without moving the first or second fingers lift the third finger off the ⑤ string and move it to the ⑥ string, third fret and play this alternate bass note. When playing G7 chord the bass and alternate bass notes are on the ⑥ and ④ strings. It is not necessary to move any of the fingers to play the alternate bass note for G7 chord.

ALTERNATE BASSES

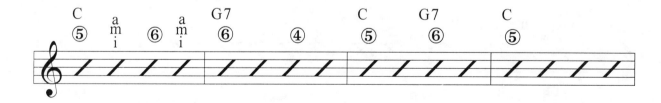

Now, you are ready to play rhythm on a real song. I have selected Skip to My Lou. I believe most people are familiar with the melody. Hum the melody or if you would like, sing the song. The chord diagram at the beginning of the song shows the starting note. The male and female voice usually overlap but, sometimes have the same range, but in any case I have shown three octaves of the starting note. Play each note and see which is easier to duplicate with your voice. If your voice is medium range you can match the note on the open ④ string. If your voice is higher try starting on the same tone as the open ①string, or, if your voice is very low try matching the open ⑥ string. Take your time, and when you are ready play the rhythm and hum, sing or think Skip to My Lou.

Let's play it first using the <u>same</u> bass notes on each chord.

VERY GOOD! Now let us play and sing "SKIP TO MY LOU" again, using **<u>ALTERNATE BASS NOTES.</u>**

HOW TO READ TABLATURE

I feel that the fastest and easiest way to learn to play the guitar is by using tablature. Tab is very easy to under-stand and transfer to the guitar. It is as easy to read and play in the high positions, such as the tenth, eleventh and twelfth frets as on the first, second and third frets.

Tablature is actually a diagram of the strings and frets of the guitar. The six lines represent the six strings, the top line being the ① st or smallest string and the bottom line the ⑥th or largest string. The numbers on the lines indicate the frets. When a number is on the top line it is on the ① st string. If it is on the second line down, it is on the ② nd string, or, if a number is on the bottom line it is on the ⑥ th string.

A 0 on a line means that string is to be played open.

REMEMBER: The lines represent the strings.
                     The numbers indicate the frets.
                     0 means open string.

The tablature is divided into measures by bar lines. There will be either four or, three counts per measure.

In the following example the first 0 is on the fourth line from the top, or, it is the ④th string plucked open. The next 0 is on the third line so, it is on the ③ rd string. The next 0 is on the ② nd string and finally, the 3 on the first, or top line indicates the 3rd fret on the ① st string.

Notice that the four numbers are spaced evenly. That shows there are four counts in the measure. Also, the counts are written below the tab. Place one of your fingers on the third fret, ①st string. Now use your thumb and begin by plucking the ④th string on the first beat (or count). Just let the thumb slide off the ④th string and come to rest against the ③rd. On the second beat pick the ③rd string by letting the thumb slide off and come to rest against the second. Pluck the ②nd string and allow the thumb to stop at the ①st. Now pick the ①st string. Remember, a finger of your left hand should be on the 3rd fret.

In the second measure the same numbers are in a vertical line. When the numbers are in a vertical line the strings are to be plucked or struck simultaneously. In this case, place your thumb on the ④ th string. Now, in one stroke, allow the thumb to quickly brush over the four strings, playing all four as close together as possible. Notice that nothing is written over the second beat so, don't play anything there. On the third beat pick the ① st string only. A finger of your left hand should be on the seventh fret. The 5 in the third measure is a single note, then on the third beat all four strings are played together as a chord.

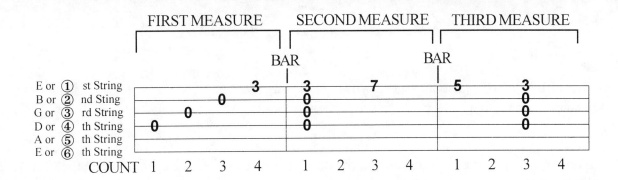

In the next study we are playing single notes, four beats to the measure. Use only the second (2nd) finger of the left hand. Use only the thumb (p) of the right hand to pick all the notes. Use the same technique as in the last study. Let the thumb slide off the string and come to rest against the next one.

Double Bar Indicates the End

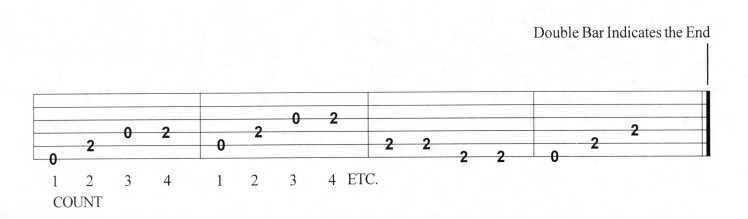

SOME NEW CHORDS

Now that you can play the melody or, lead, you need to learn some new chords so that you can play the accompaniment or, rhythm guitar part. We will talk about chords just momentarily before we begin the next study.

When you play a new chord, pick each string individually and listen for buzzes and dead or muffled strings. If a string buzzes it is probably because your finger is not close enough to the fret or, you are not pressing the string tightly enough. Try moving the finger closer to the fret and press the string tightly against it.

If a string is deadened it is probably because one of your fingers is touching it. You might check to see if a finger is leaning against a string it is not supposed to touch. If so, try bending the finger a bit more and make the necessary adjustments. Remember to use the fingertips and keep the fingers arched.

Your fingertips may become slightly sore, but this is normal. It happens to almost everyone when he/she begins learning to play the guitar. Just keep on pickin' and the soreness will leave in a few days when your fingertips begin to toughen.

Okay. The new chords are E, A, and B7. Play alternate bass notes and remember to play the bass on the first and third beats. Use the (i), m, a fingers to pluck the ①st, ②nd and ③rd strings all together on the second and fourth beats. Okay, here we go 1 2 3 4.

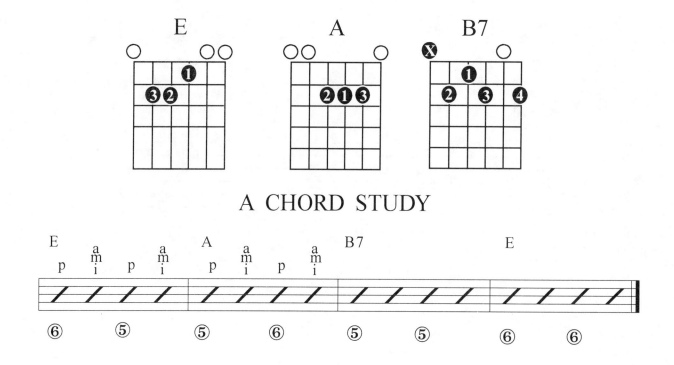

A CHORD STUDY

24

THE BLUES PROGRESSION

The next solo utilizes the same fingering and picking, as the last study on page 23, i.e., the middle finger of the left hand and the right thumb. The chord changes are a standard progression called the twelve bar blues progression. This progression is also used for boogies, and many '50s rock and country songs. We will discuss this further in a later chapter. Let's give this tune a title. I think I will call it the "Walking Blues."

WALKING BLUES

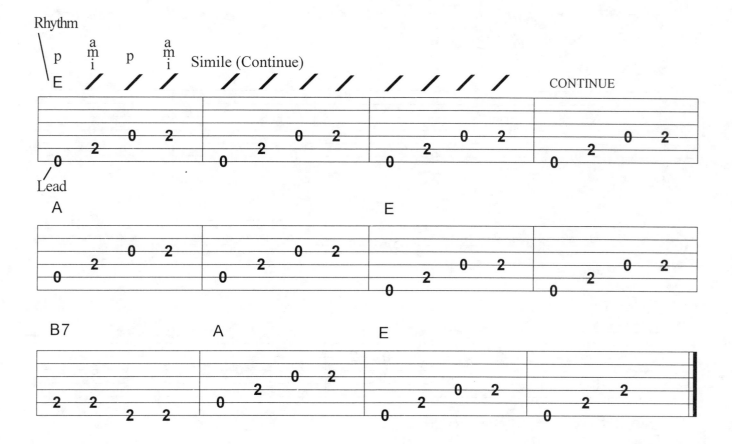

From this point on, the standard music notation will be written above the tablature for those people who read music, but are learning fingerstyle. We will discuss reading music in a later chapter, but for now notice; there is a music note directly above each number in the tablature, which is on the same beat. The chord symbols are written above the music. When playing accompaniment (rhythm guitar), begin where the first chord symbol appears and continue playing the correct number of beats per measure until you come to the next symbol, then change to the new chord, etc. Also, the time *signature appears at the beginning of the music. The picking pattern is written above the music indicating which fingers to use. When you feel comfortable with the melody, then play the rhythm a few times. You need to be able to play either part.

WALKING BLUES

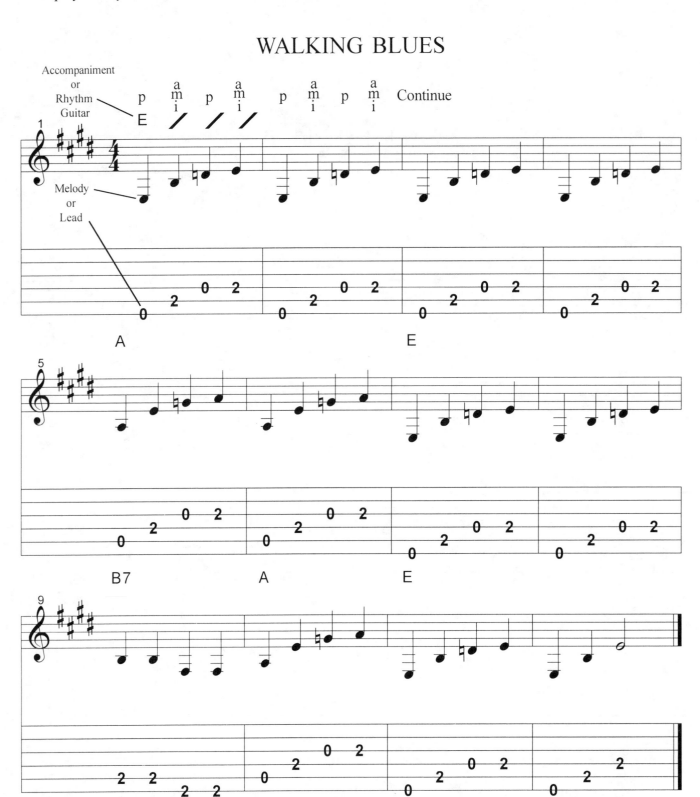

*See Time Signature on the next page.

26

While reading music is not necessary to use this book, you will need to learn some symbols and words so we can communicate. You will need to learn such things as time signatures (whether there are three or four counts per measure), keys, so you will know what key you are in, tempo (rate of speed), repeat signs, which section is to be repeated, verse, chorus, bridge etc.

THE TIME SIGNATURE

FOUR-FOUR	COMMON TIME	THREE FOUR or THREE QUARTER
four counts per measure	same as four four	3 counts per measure
$\frac{4}{4}$	𝄴	$\frac{3}{4}$

D.C. al Fine means to repeat from beginning to the word Fine (the end).

(A)   Fine   (B)   D.C.

(ABA) ← Play in this order.

D.S. al Fine means to repeat from the sign 𝄋 to the word Fine.

(A)   𝄋   (B)   Fine   (C)

(ABCB)

Two dots before a double bar means to return to the beginning
or to another double bar followed by two dots.

(A)   (B)

(AABB)

First and second endings are often used after repetitions in music.

First ending   Second ending

(A)   1. (B)   2. (C)

(ABAC)

TWO NEW CHORDS

Em **Am**

The small "m" after a chord tells you the chord is a "minor" chord. The new chords on this page are E minor and A minor.

$$\frac{3}{4}$$ or THREE FOUR time

Up to this point everything you have played has been four counts per measure, or $\frac{4}{4}$ time. The time signature tells you there are three counts per measure.

In the following study you will use the new chords, playing them in time. On the first beat pick the bass string with your thumb, then, on the second and third beats pluck the ③rd, ②nd and ① st strings with your fingers.

```
        BASS-PLUCK-PLUCK    BASS-PLUCK-PLUCK
OR      1     2     3       1     2     3
```

A NEW PICKING PATTERN

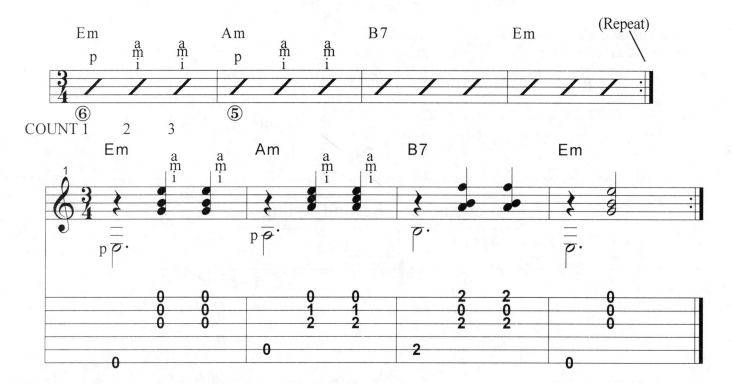

PLAYING BETWEEN THE BEATS
(eighth notes)

When we play on every beat we are playing quarter notes. When we play on every beat and also play a note between the beats we are playing eighth notes. The following pattern or lick is in eighth-note rhythm. Count "1 & 2 & 3 & 4 &" and space the counts evenly. Use the thumb (p) and pick the bass ⑤th string on the first beat and use the m and a fingers to pluck the ②nd and ①st strings on the second beat. Again, using the p, pick the bass ④th string on the third beat and again using the m and a fingers pluck the ②nd and ①st strings on the fourth beat. Now, play this pattern again and using the (i) finger pick the ③rd string on the "&" (and) between the counts.

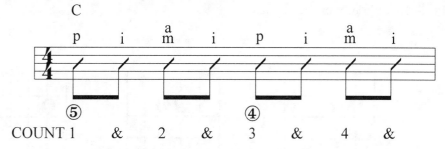

Play this pattern several times or, until you feel relaxed before going to the next solo.

The next pattern is in $\frac{3}{4}$ time. Use the p and pick the bass ⑤th string on the first beat. Use the m and a fingers to pluck the ②nd and ①st strings on the second and third beats. Use the (i) finger to pick the ③ string on the "&" between the counts.

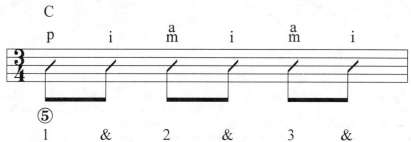

An easy way to "feel" the eighth-note rhythm is to "pat" your foot on the beats. Play the pattern and tap your foot against the floor on the counts, and raise the foot on the "&" (ands).

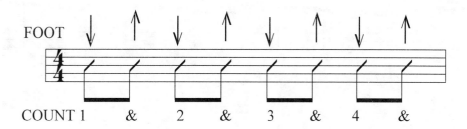

A VERY USEFUL PICKING PATTERN
AND
A CHORD PROGRESSION USED FOR MANY SONGS

Notice that when changing C, Em and Am chords the middle (2) finger remains on the ④th string. This makes the changes much easier by anchoring the hand in position on the strings. You may need to make some slight adjustment of the hand, but the finger stays on the string. This is just one little trick you need to remember that makes playing the guitar fun. Always change chords this way whenever possible. Another thing to remember is: When changing positions or chords, always keep the fingers as close to the strings as possible. The further you move your hand from the fingerboard the faster you have to move to get to the next chord. Just glide over the strings.

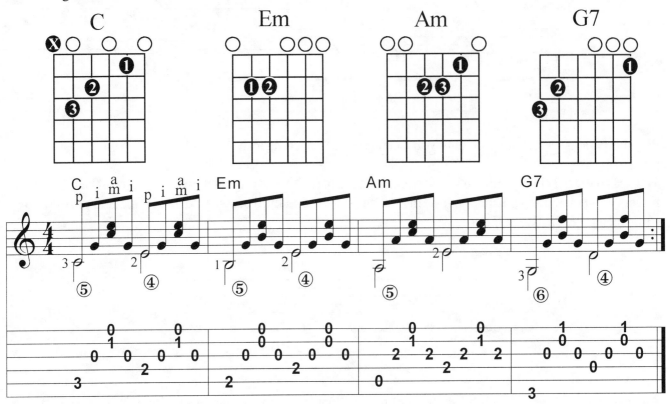

COUNT 1 & 2 & 3 & 4 &

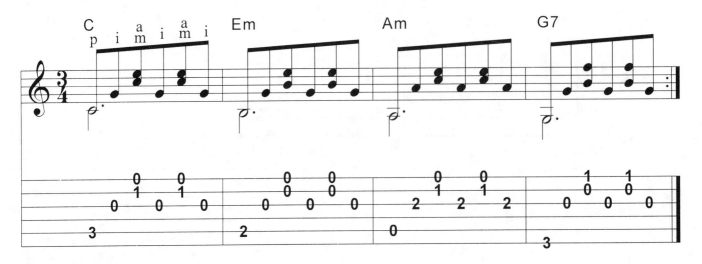

COUNT 1 & 2 & 3 &

PLAYING MELODY AND ACCOMPANIMENT AT THE SAME TIME

A very important and pleasing feature of fingerstyle guitar is, that two or more parts can be played simultaneously. Having the ability to play melody, harmony, rhythm and bass at the same time is an attribute of the experienced fingerstyle guitarist. Many guitarists in jazz, classical and country are capable of and do play concerts alone. Merle Travis usually performed alone and is at the top of the list. He was one of the world's greatest guitarists and entertainers. Thom Bresh works alone and is a superb guitarist and performer, the complete entertainer. Chet Atkins plays some very impressive solos doing all the parts. The Scottish jazz guitarist Martin Taylor is incredible. He plays a moving four-four bass line with his thumb while playing comp (accompaniment) with his index and middle fingers and, at the same time playing melody and improvising with his ring and little fingers. All this at lightning fast tempos, much like a jazz combo such as the Oscar Peterson Trio (Oscar Peterson, piano, Ray Brown, bass and Herb Ellis, guitar) sounded.

THUMBING IT

Okay! Let's do it! Notice that "Thumbing It" is in 3/4 time. First, you need to learn the thumb pattern. Form C chord and hold it throughout the first two measures. Place your right thumb on the ⑤th string and pluck it on the first beat. Then pick the ④th string on the second beat and the ③rd string on the third beat. Change to G7 and again, using only the thumb, pluck the ⑥th, ⑤th and ④th strings. Play this pattern a few times or until you can change from C to G7 and back to C while holding a steady, even tempo.

THUMBING IT

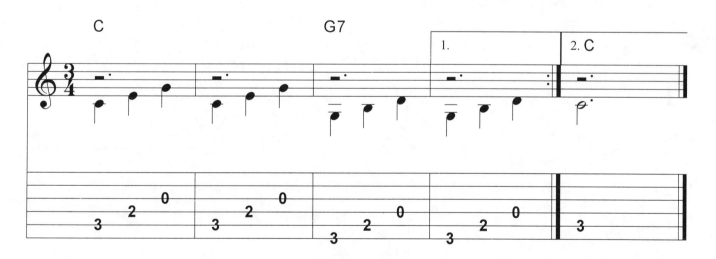

COUNT   1   2   3

The thumb plays the same pattern on "The Only One" as it did on the last study. While holding C chord, pick the ① st string with your m finger on the first beat, at the same time you pick the ⑤ th string with your thumb. Continue the accompaniment pattern with your thumb and then, in the second measure, pick the ② nd string with your (i) finger on the first beat, at the same time you pick the ⑤ th string with your thumb. Change to G7 and use the same method of picking. Play "The Only One" until you can change chords, keep time and feel relaxed before going to the next solo.

THE ONLY ONE

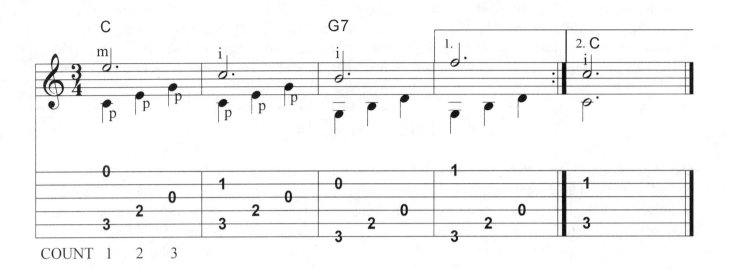

COUNT 1   2   3

In "Three In One" the thumb again plays the same pattern. The fingers play on the first and third beats. As usual, play this tune until you feel comfortable.

THREE IN ONE

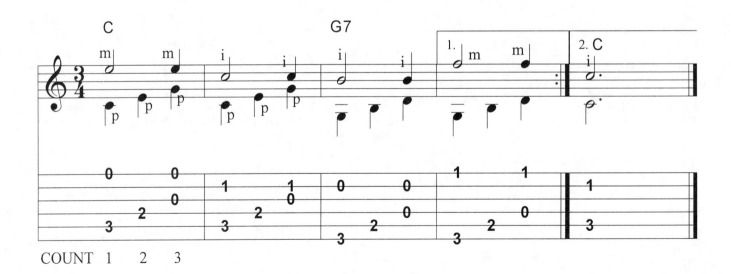

COUNT 1   2   3

The fingers play the same pattern throughout. The m finger picks the ① st string on the first beat and the i finger picks the ② nd string on the second beat.

GETTING GOOD

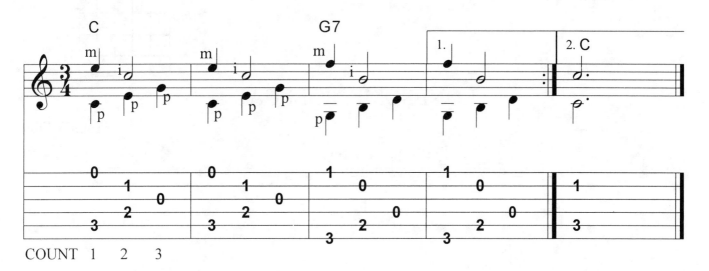

COUNT 1   2   3

Now you are ready to play on every beat with both the thumb and fingers. The pattern is very much like the last one; we have just added a note on the third beat. The picking pattern is m, i, m on the ①st, ②nd, and ①st strings, except the last note in the fourth measure is in the ②nd string.

GETTING BETTER

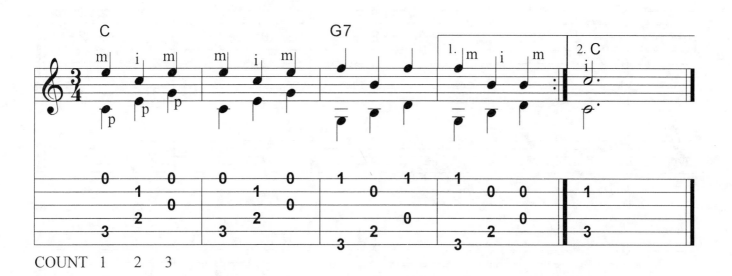

COUNT 1   2   3

33

The following solo is in the same style as the studies on the
previous two pages. The interesting chord progression
changes the dark mood of the minor chords to a lighter, brighter
mood by changing to major chords, then, goes back to the
somber minor chords.

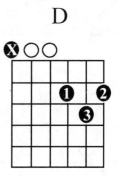

LONESOME POLECAT

Tommy Flint

HITTING ON ALL FOUR

Hitting ON ALL FOUR is in common (four-four) time. The middle and index fingers play the melody line and the thumb plays a simple accompaniment. Notice that the middle finger and thumb pluck the strings at the same time on the first and third beats. The middle finger alternates between the ① st and ② nd strings (the ① st on the first beat and the ② nd on the third beat).

The thumb plucks the ⑤ th string on the first beat and the ④ th string on the third beat in C chord. In G7 chord the thumb plucks the ⑥ th and ④ th strings.

The index finger plucks the ③ rd string on the second and fourth beats. Play this study until you feel comfortable with it before going to the next one.

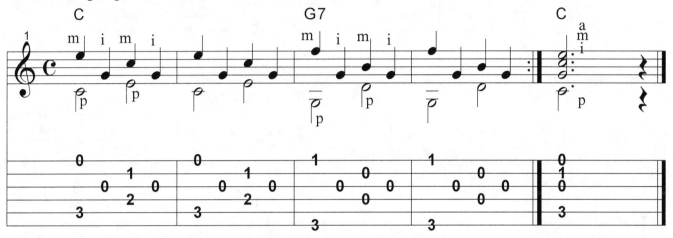

COUNT 1   2   3   4

THE SECOND TIME

In "The Second Time" the picking is very much like the last study. We are still using C and G7 chords, however, you will use the fourth (little) finger to add melody notes to the chords. In the first measure, use the fourth finger on the third fret, ② nd string and in the second measure, use the same finger on the third fret, ① st string. Then, leave the fourth finger on the ① st string and change the other fingers to G7 chord. Again, use the fourth finger on the ② nd and ① st strings for the notes on the third fret.

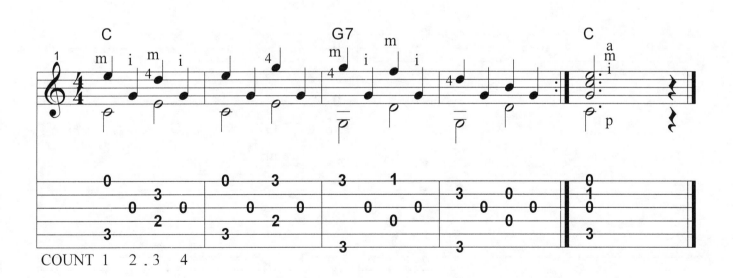

COUNT 1   2 . 3   4

The solo on this page is basically the same style you have been playing. Alternate the middle and index fingers on the melody while your thumb plays the bass line. There is a slight difference in measures seven and fifteen. The index finger plucks the ①st and ②nd strings instead of the third.

IN THE EARLY MORNING MIST

This is played in the same style, but notice in measure seven, the (i) finger picks the ②nd string on the fourth beat. And, <u>you have a new chord</u>.

A7

ON THE APPALACHIAN TRAIL

Tommy Flint

You're doing great. In the following study we are adding a couple of notes with the thumb. Form C chord and use the thumb to pluck the ⑤ th string on the first and third beats. Then, on the second and fourth beats, pluck the ④ th string with the thumb, at the same time your index finger picks the ③rd string. Hold C chord and play this pattern a few times before moving on. Now change to G7 chord and pick the ⑥ th string on the first and third beats and again using the index finger and thumb pick the ③ rd and ④ th strings on the second and fourth beats. Play this pattern changing from C to G 7 until you can hold a steady tempo, then go to the following study. We are adding notes with the middle finger on the first and third beats. The pattern is middle finger and thumb index finger and thumb, middle finger and thumb, index finger and thumb.

THE BLUESTEM SLOPES

Tommy Flint

38

USING THE THUMB ON ALL FOUR BEATS
AND A NEW CHORD

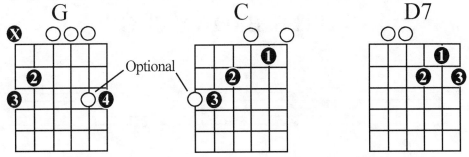

G   C   D7

Optional

Play, G and D7 using the rhythms (picking patterns) you have learned up to this point. When you feel comfortable with the new chord, let us begin this new style. Make G chord, then pluck the ⑥th string on the first beat, the ④th string on the second beat, ⑥th the third beat and the ④th string again on the fourth beat. Change to C chord and repeat the pattern except, pluck the ⑤th string on the first and third beats. Repeat this on D7.

STEPPING OUT

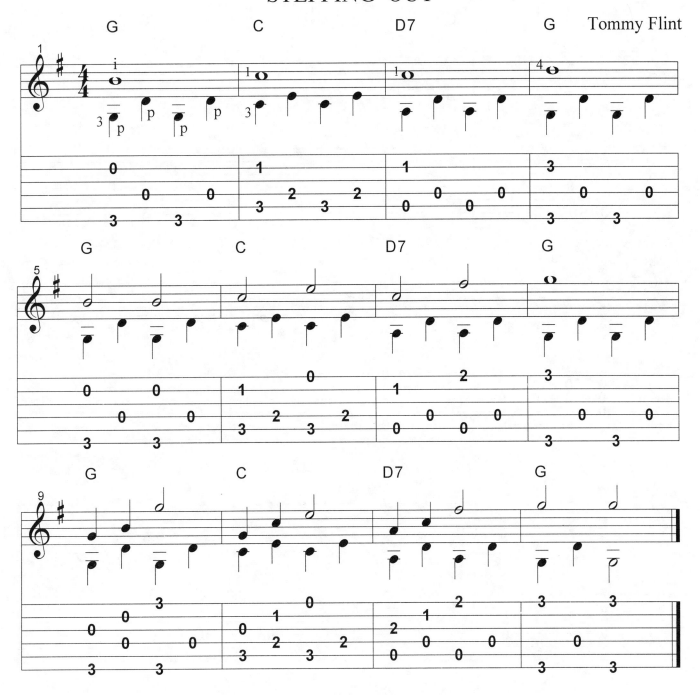

Tommy Flint

The thumb again plucks on all four beats throughout Little Brown Jug. Notice, in the second measure, C chord is used on the first two beats, but changes to A7 for the last two beats. Also, in the ninth and thirteenth measures, full chord forms are not used, and you will pick three or four strings at the same time. The thumb continues to play on all four beats.

LITTLE BROWN JUG

Again, on this page your thumb will play on all four beats. However, you will play alternate bass notes. Remember how you played alternate basses when you played rhythm on page 20? This is very similar except you play a melody line with the finger instead of plucking three strings.

Here is the thumb pattern for C chord:
p p p p
⑤④⑥④
count 1 2 3 4

D9

THE FIERY SKIPPER

Tommy Flint

EIGHTH NOTES IN THE MELODY LINE

There is an "and" after the count of two through the first eight measures. The melody notes are played on 1 2&. There are no melody notes on three and four. The thumb plays on all four beats. In the ninth, eleventh, thirteenth and fourteenth measures, the melody notes are played on 1 2 3&. Use the picking indicated until you feel comfortable and relaxed.

LUNA'S TUNE

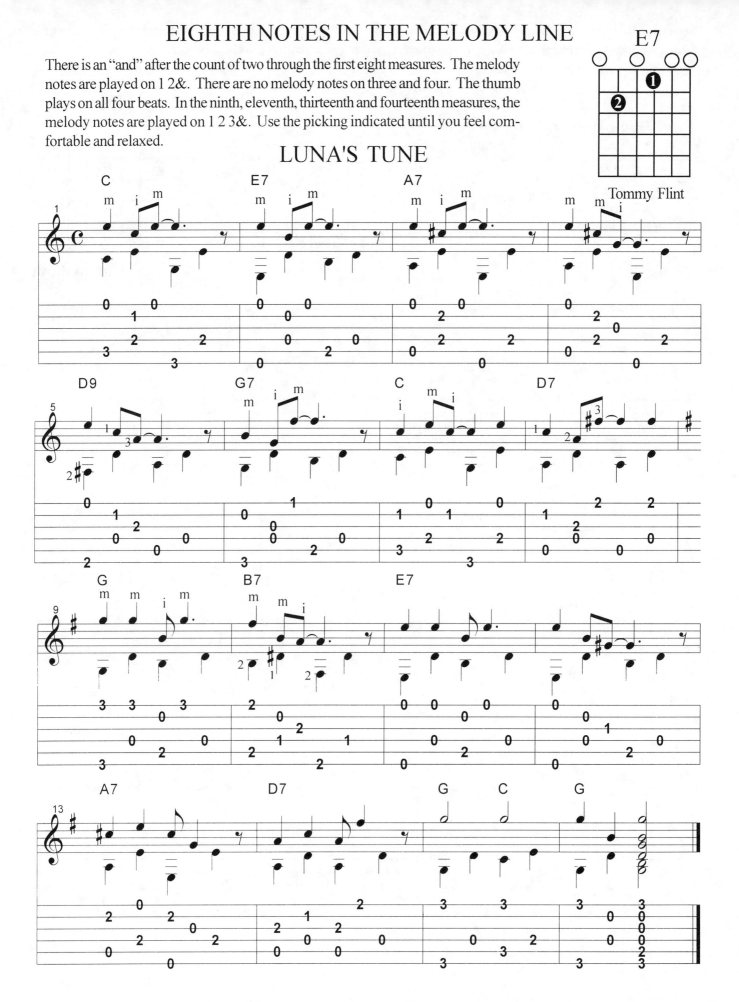

Tommy Flint

PICK-UP NOTES

Some songs do not begin on the first beat. One or more notes at the beginning of a piece of music, before the first full measure, are referred to as pick-up notes. In the following solo the first pick-up is on "and" after the count of three. Count "1 & 2 & 3" then play the pick-ups on "& 4 &." When you play the accompaniment or rhythm, start on the first beat, first measure. Use the indicated picking until you feel comfortable and confident.

HE'S GOT THE WHOLE WORLD IN HIS HANDS

Tommy Flint

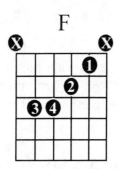

F

It is very easy to change from C chord to this form of F. Make C chord. Leave your first and third fingers on the ②nd and ⑤th strings. Move the second finger from the ④th string to the ③rd string, second fret, then, place the fourth finger on the ④th string, third fret. Practice changing from C to F a few times, then let's play.

SNAP CRACKLE, CRACKLE and BANG

Tommy Flint

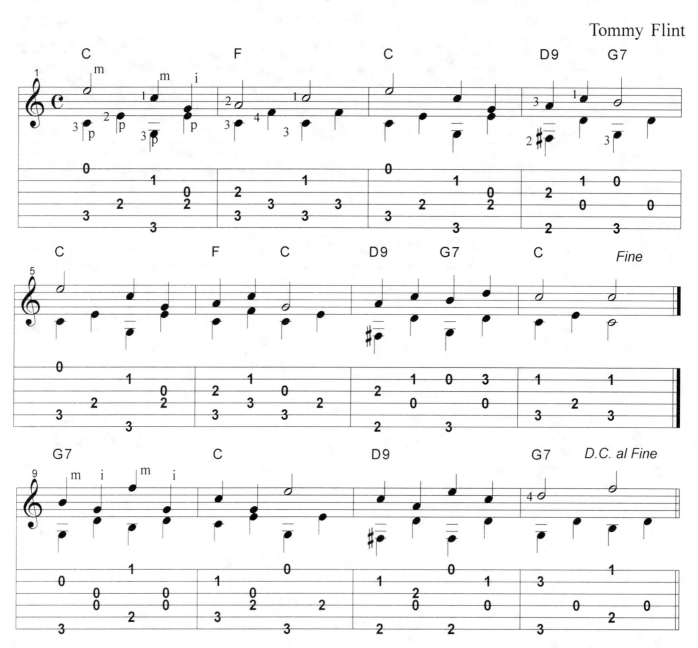

D.C. al Fine: Return to Beginning and Play to Fine.

44

THE FIRST BARRE (BAR)

Up to this point you have used the fingertips to depress the strings on all chords. Now, we are going to break that rule and lay the finger flat on two strings. You will soon see how useful this technique can be.

Use the first finger and while keeping the first joint (joint closest to the fingertip) straight, lay the finger flat on the ①st and ②nd strings at the first fret.

Work with this fingering until you can·get a good, clear tone on both strings, then move the same finger to the third fret, then to the fifth fret, etc.

Next, begin at the first fret and pick the strings on the counts of one and two, then move to the second fret on three and four, the third fret on one and two, the fourth fret on three and four, etc. Continue this exercise until you reach the twelfth fret, then, move in reverse until you get back to the first fret. You will be amazed at how soon this becomes very easy for you.

Okay, now that you can barre two strings, let's add another note. Again, using the first finger, barre the ①st and ②nd strings at the first fret. Next, place the tip of the second finger on the ③rd string, second fret. Remember, keep the first finger flat and don't bend the first joint.

Play this chord from the first fret to the twelfth fret and back to the first. This is F chord.

ANOTHER F CHORD

F

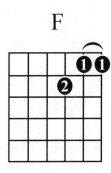

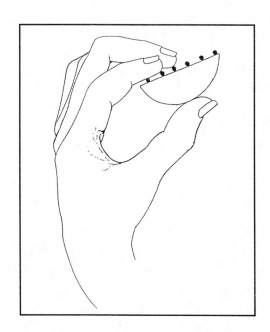

THE HALF BARRE (BAR)

When you lay your finger flat on more than one string, this is called a barre (bar). To execute the half barre, place the first finger flat on the ① st, ② nd and ③ rd strings, being careful not to bend the first joint. Keep your thumb on the back of the neck and allow your wrist to hang in a relaxed position. Don't let the palm of your hand touch the back of the neck. This is a half barre and will be indicated C 1/2. (If you place the first finger flat on all six strings without bending the first or second joints, you are making a full bar. It will be indicated by C). The barre sign will usually be followed by a roman numeral that specifies the fret to barre.

C 1/2 V tells you to form a half barre at the fifth fret, or, C1/2 IX tells you to make a half barre at the ninth fret.

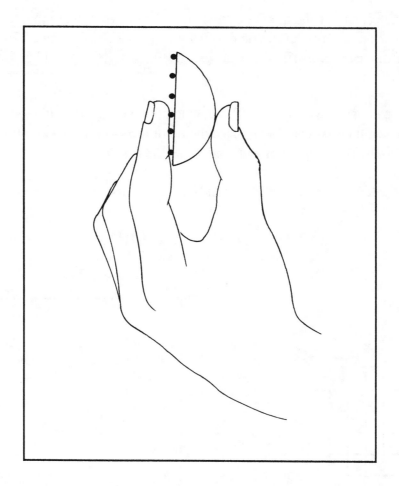

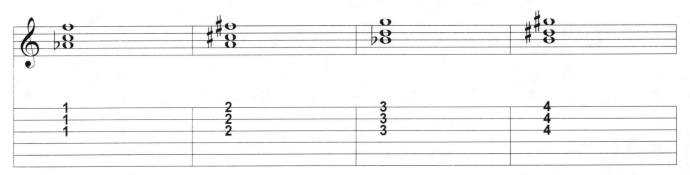

TWO NEW CHORDS

You will find these these chords to be very useful, because they have no open strings and can be played in any position. Form the three finger F chord you learned on page 45. Now, place the tip of your third finger on the④th string, third fret. Play this chord in all positions until you feel comfortable with it, but remember it is F at the first fret.

When changing from C to F chord, don't lift the first finger off the ②nd string, just straighten it at the first joint, and allow it to lie flat on the ②nd and ①st strings. While keeping the second and first fingers together, lift them just enough to move them from the ⑤th and ④th strings to the ④th and ③rd.

Keep changing from C to F until it is easy for you and you will feel a great sense of accomplishment.

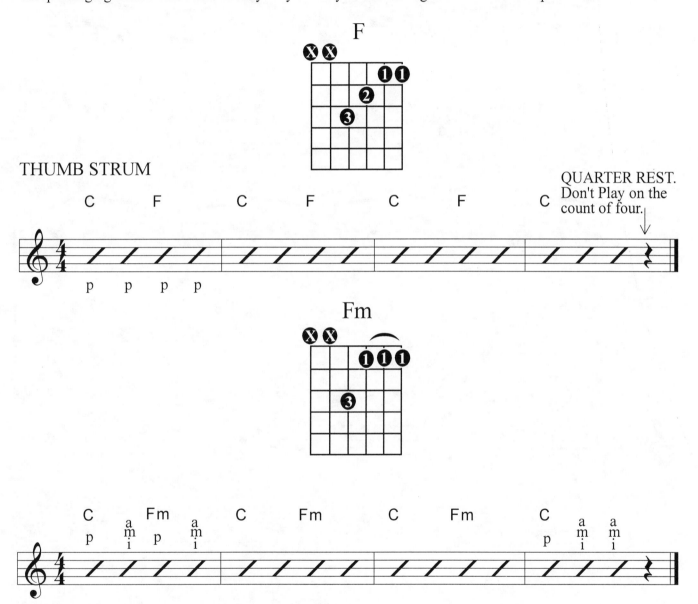

USING THE HALF BARRE

The G minor chord in the second measure is a half barre at the third fret. After forming the barre, pick the ③rd, ②nd and ①st strings, then while holding the barre, place the fourth finger on the fifth fret, ①st string and pluck that note.

ALBERT LEA ANN

Tommy Flint

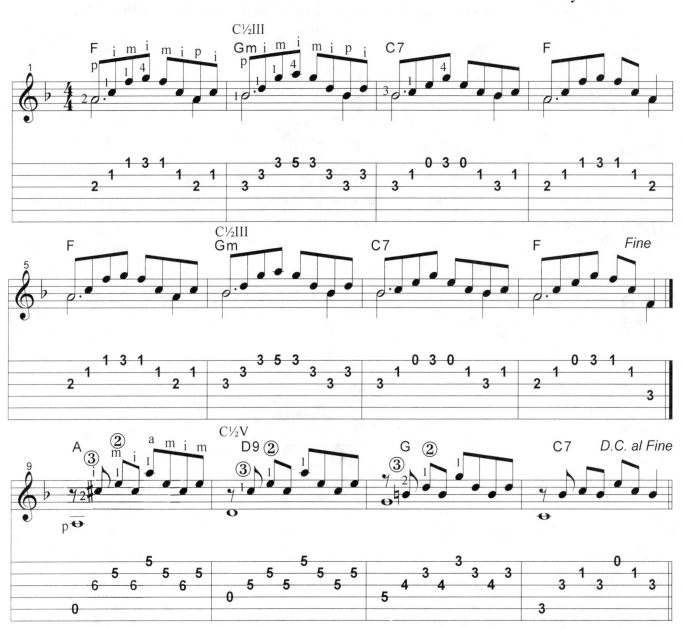

RIDING OUT OF DODGE

Tommy Flint

The first two lines of the following solo are played in the eighth note style as explained on page 27. Measures 9 through 14 are also in eighth note rhythm, but a different picking pattern. The *m* finger and *p* (thumb) pluck at the same time on the first beat. Then the *(i)* finger plucks the ② string, the *p* plucks the ③ string and the *(i)* again plucks the ② string. The last half of the measure repeats this pattern. Measure 15 goes back to the original pattern.

SOME CHORDS YOU NEED TO LEARN
USE THIS PAGE AS A REFERENCE CHART

MAJOR CHORDS

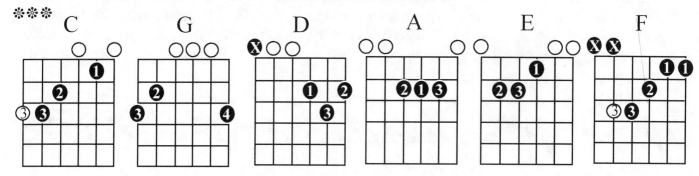

SEVENTH CHORDS

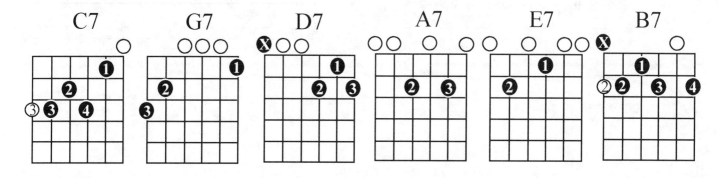

MINOR CHORDS

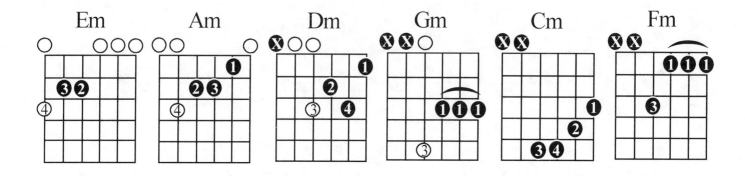

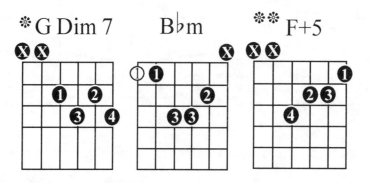

* Dim. or a O indicates "Diminished."

** The Plus sign + signifies "Augmented" 5th

*** Circle with white background and black number denotes an "optional" fingering

Pick out any letter on the circle as the tonic, or 1 chord. Now, move counterclockwise one letter. This is the subdominant or 4 chord. Next, move clockwise from the tonic one letter and this is the dominant or 5 chord. The dominant chord should be a seventh in most cases. As an example, the three principal chords in the key of C are: C-F-G7 or, in the key of G, the chords are: G-C-D7.

Remember, find the tonic on the circle and the subdominant and dominant 7th are counterclockwise and clockwise.

Every major key has a relative *minor* key. The letters inside the circle are the relative minors. In a minor key the tonic or 1, and the subdominant or 4 are minor chords and the dominant or 5 is a seventh chord. So, in the key of A minor, the three principal chords are: AM-Dm-E7. In the key of Fm: Fm-B♭m-C7.

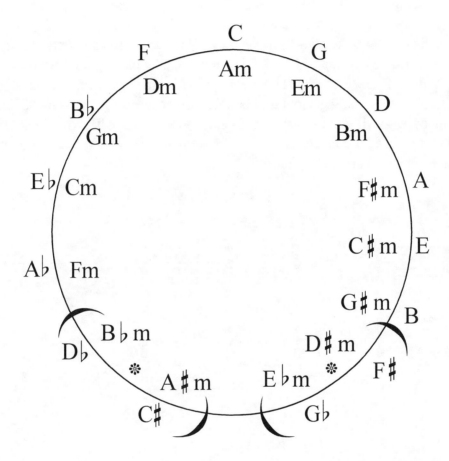

* The Fingering for D♭ and C♯ is identical. G♭ and F♯ are identical.

ALTERNATE BASS NOTES

Sometimes the same bass note sustained through a chord progression (pedal note) is beautiful and effective but, sometimes, hearing the same bass note played many times in succession, even on the same chord, can become extremely boring. By using alternate bass notes the accompaniment sometimes becomes more flowing and much more interesting.

The studies on this page demonstrate how to use the root and alternate basses. It is sometimes necessary to lift a finger off a bass string and move it to a different string, such as C chord. The root note is on the ⑤th string. To play the alternate bass, lift the finger off the ⑤th string and move it to the ⑥th. This is not necessary on other chords such as A. The root note is the ⑤th and the alternate bass is on the ⑥th string.

In the following studies we are using the THREE PRINCIPAL CHORDS in five major keys and four *minor* keys. The principal chords are the most commonly used chords in a key. They are built on the I, IV and V degrees of the scale. You will learn the scales in a succeeding chapter. For now, just play the chords using alternate basses and learn the three chords in each key. Don't try to memorize the chords by studying the page without your instrument. Rather, absorb this knowledge by playing these studies on your guitar and calling the chord names aloud. Performing with your guitar is different from reading about it, just as flying an airplane is different from reading about it. I believe you become a guitarist by "doing." As your brain absorbs this knowledge so will your fingers, hands and entire body. When you think C, your fingers will go to that chord. It becomes automatic, a reflex. And, soon you can play the guitar much as you speak. It will become less mechanical and more fluid.

KEY OF C

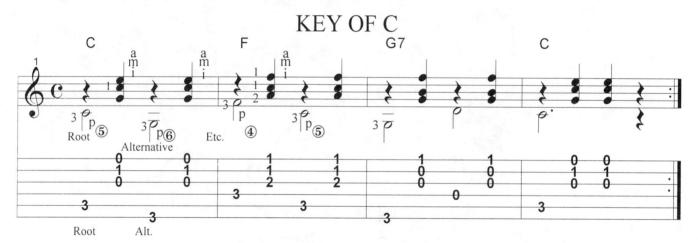

KEY OF G

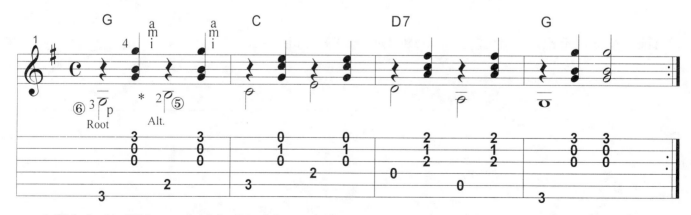

* This is the III instead of the V of the scale

I, IV and V IN VARIOUS KEYS AND RHYTHMS
KEY OF D

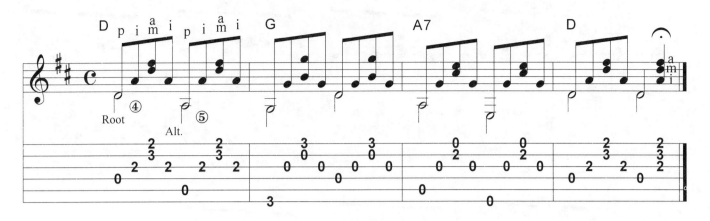

KEY OF A

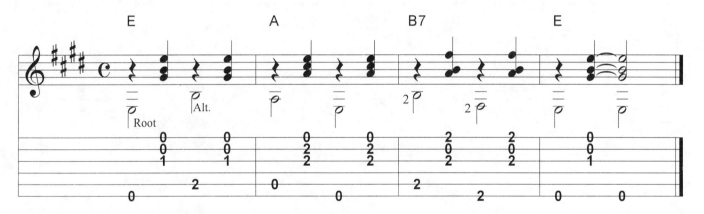

KEY OF E

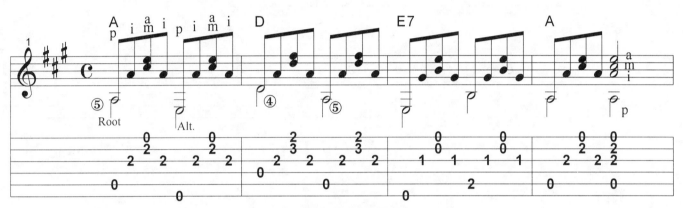

KEY OF Am

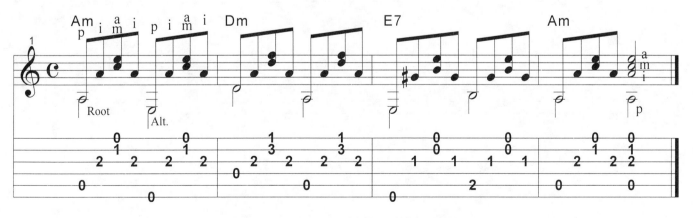

KEY OF Em

KEY OF Dm

KEY OF Fm

LONELY GUITAR

Use p, i, m, a PICKING PATTERN. The left hand should remain on the chords.

BURY ME BENEATH THE WILLOW
KEY OF D

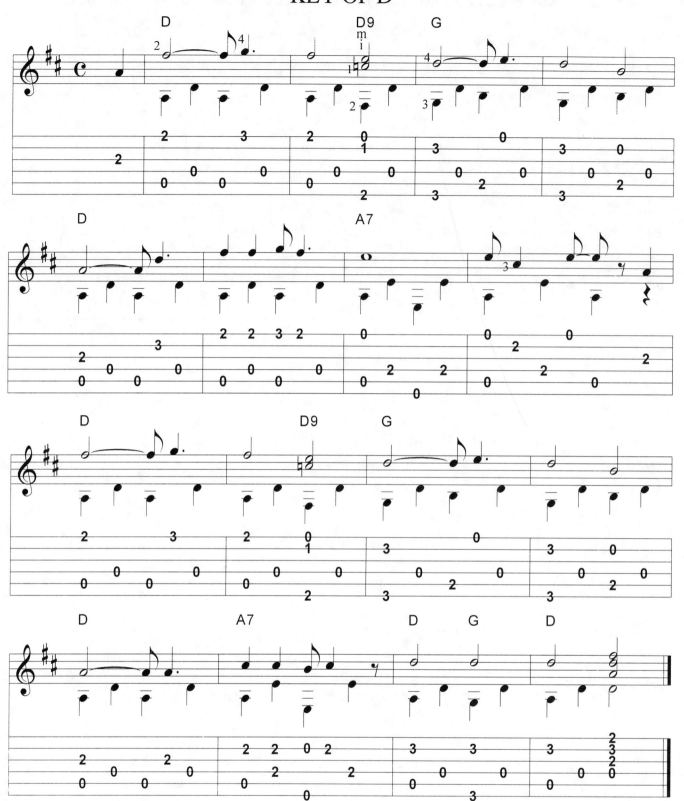

TRIPLETS

The triplet is a group of three notes played in the time of two notes of the same kind. The triplets on this page are eighth note triplets. As you know there are two eighth notes on each beat, spaced evenly. To play eighth note triplets, play three notes, spaced evenly on each beat. Tap your foot on the counts, and count "one-trip-let, two-trip-let, three-trip-let, four-trip-let."

Triplets will usually be indicated by the number three and a bracket above or below the notes.

EIGHTH NOTES

TRIPLETS

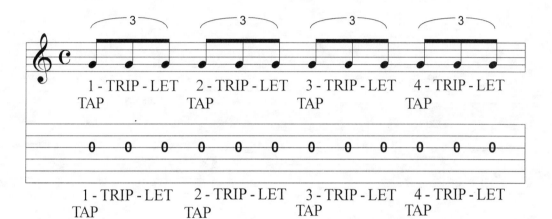

A TRIPLET STUDY

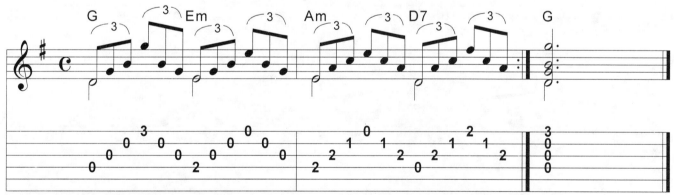

1 TRIPLET 2 TRIPLET 3 TRIPLET 4 TRIPLET

TAP   TAP   TAP   TAP

HOUSE OF THE RISING SUN

WHAT KEY AM I IN?

Most melodies end on the first note of the scale and the root note of the tonic, or I (one) chord of the key in which they are written. In other words, if a song ends with G chord and the last note is G, you are in the key of G. Or, if the last note and chord are E and Em, you are in the key of E minor.

KEY SIGNATURES

When you look at a song book or a page of sheet music the key signature tells you the key the song is in. So, at this point you need to learn some more signs.

This is a Treble Clef: 𝄞 . The clef determines the names of the lines and spaces of the staff. Almost all guitar music is written on the staff using the Treble Clef. The clef sign appears at the beginning of each staff.

This is a sharp sign: ♯   This is a flat sign: ♭

The number of sharps or flats after the clef sign determines the key. The key of C and the relative minor key of A minor have no sharps or flats in the key signature. One sharp sign is the key of G, or E minor, the relative minor key. Below is a chart of key signatures, showing major and minor keys.

SHARPS

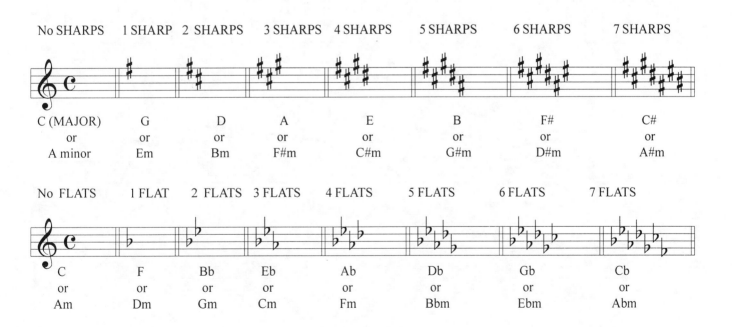

No SHARPS	1 SHARP	2 SHARPS	3 SHARPS	4 SHARPS	5 SHARPS	6 SHARPS	7 SHARPS
C (MAJOR)	G	D	A	E	B	F#	C#
or	or	or	or	or	or	or	or
A minor	Em	Bm	F#m	C#m	G#m	D#m	A#m

No FLATS	1 FLAT	2 FLATS	3 FLATS	4 FLATS	5 FLATS	6 FLATS	7 FLATS
C	F	Bb	Eb	Ab	Db	Gb	Cb
or	or	or	or	or	or	or	or
Am	Dm	Gm	Cm	Fm	Bbm	Ebm	Abm

THINGS TO REMEMBER

There are only seven letters in the musical alphabet:

A B C D E F G

(These can be altered by sharps or flats but we will wait until later to discuss that.) There are several octaves (the same note in higher or lower pitches) of each note on the guitar.

┌─first octave─┐   ┌─second octave─┐
│ A B C D E F G │   │ A B C D E F G │

Each time a sharp is added to the key signature, the key moves a fifth. If you count A as I (one), then B is II (two), C is III (three), D is IV (four), etc.

The tones of the C scale are:

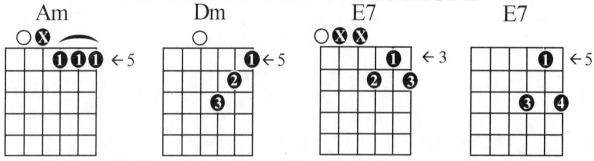

I	II	III	IV	V	VI	VII		Second	Octave				
C	D	E	F	G	A	B		C	D	E	F	G	A B

The key of C has no sharps or flats, remember? One sharp moves the key a fifth which is G. When we add another sharp G will be counted as one, so we will have to use the two octaves to find the key of two sharps. Since there are only seven letters in the musical alphabet, after G, we start on the second octave and continue until we reach the fifth, which is D.

After B, when we move a fifth, we add a sharp to the letter name. A fifth above B is F♯. A fifth above F♯ is C♯. When a flat sign is added we move a fourth. When C is one, F is the fourth, so one flat is the key of F. When there is more than one flat in the key signature, we also add a flat to the letter name. Two flats is the key of B♭, three flats is the key of E♭, etc.

THE CHORDS USED FOR PRELUDE

A MINOR STUDY

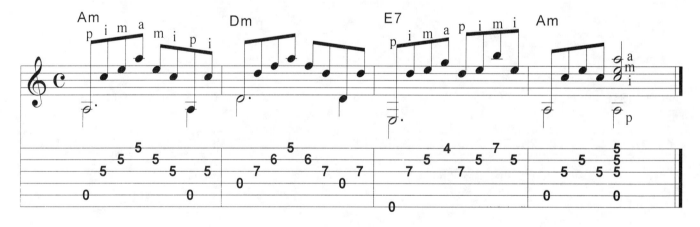

PRELUDE

Play Legato (Hold Chords)
USE HALF BAR IN MEASURES 1, 4, 5, 8, 9, 12, 13 AND 16.

Moderato

Tommy Flint

SYNCOPATION

I think one of the exciting things about fingerstyle guitar is the lively, spontaneous feel of the melody floating, dancing and doing its own thing above a solid, steady rhythm and bass, which holds it all together. The melody notes are like scouts going out to explore, to find beauty and meaning, but always reporting back to headquarters, the rhythm and bass, for the discoveries to be assimilated. Syncopation is a tool that will help you achieve this feel. Syncopation is irregularity of rhythm, or placing the accents on beats which are usually unaccented.

When you play the first example below, simply alternate the thumb and finger. The thumb plays on all four beats, but the fingers play only on the "ands" after one, two and three. There is nothing after the fourth beat. p i p m p i

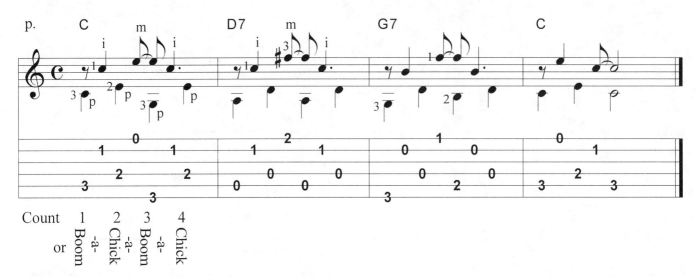

The following exercise is a two-measure pattern. The easiest way to count the two measures is "Boom-Chick-A-Boom-a-Chick-a-Boom-a-Chick-a-Boom-Chick." Again it is possible to use the index finger only; however, I suggest the two-finger picking.

The count is the same in this pattern as in the preceding exercise. Nevertheless, it is imperative that you use the thumb and two-finger style because there are more than two consecutive eighth notes in the melody line.

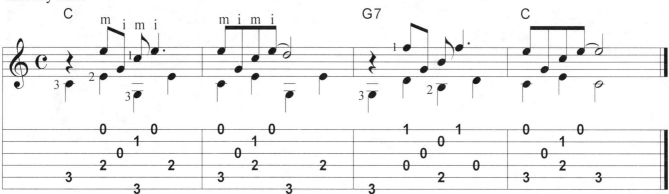

BLUE RIVER TRAIN

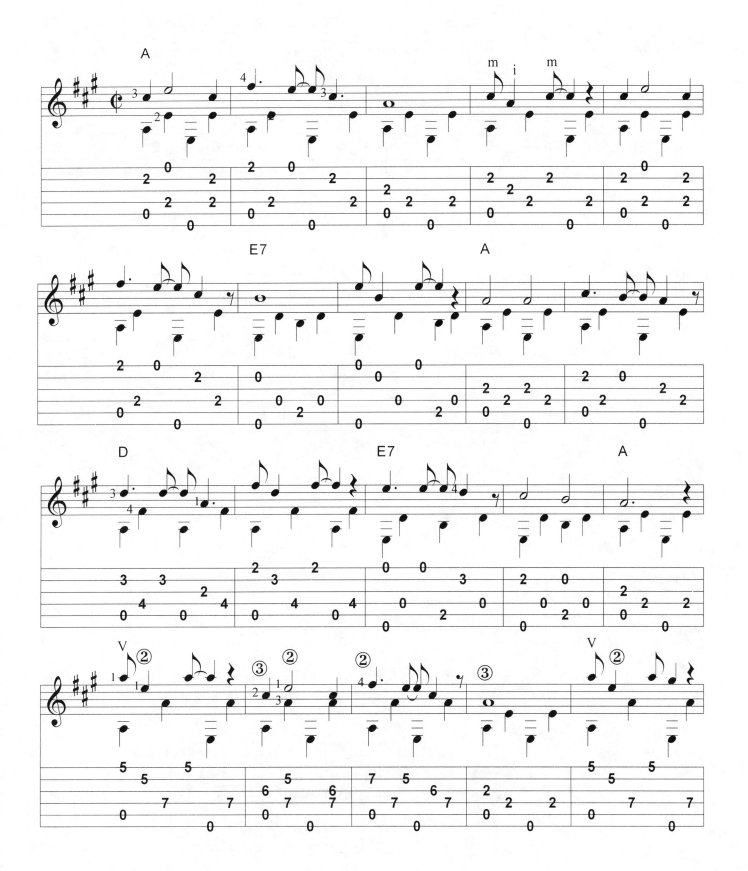

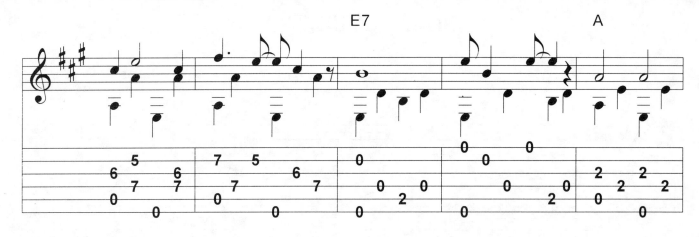

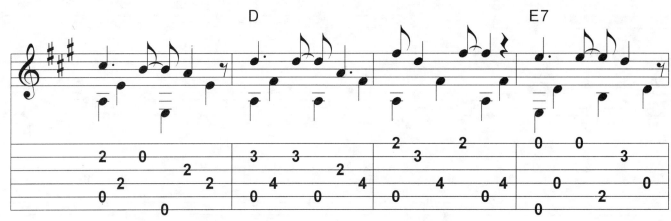

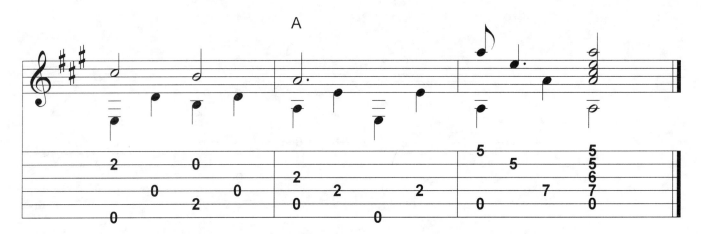

SOME NEW CHORDS USED IN "BLUE RIVER TRAIN"

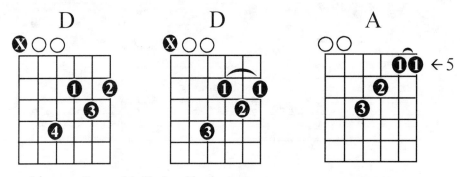

Learn to finger this D chord both ways.

POWDER HOUSE BLUES

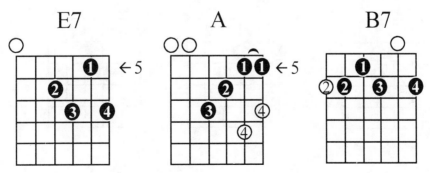

QUAKER NOTES

Tommy Flint

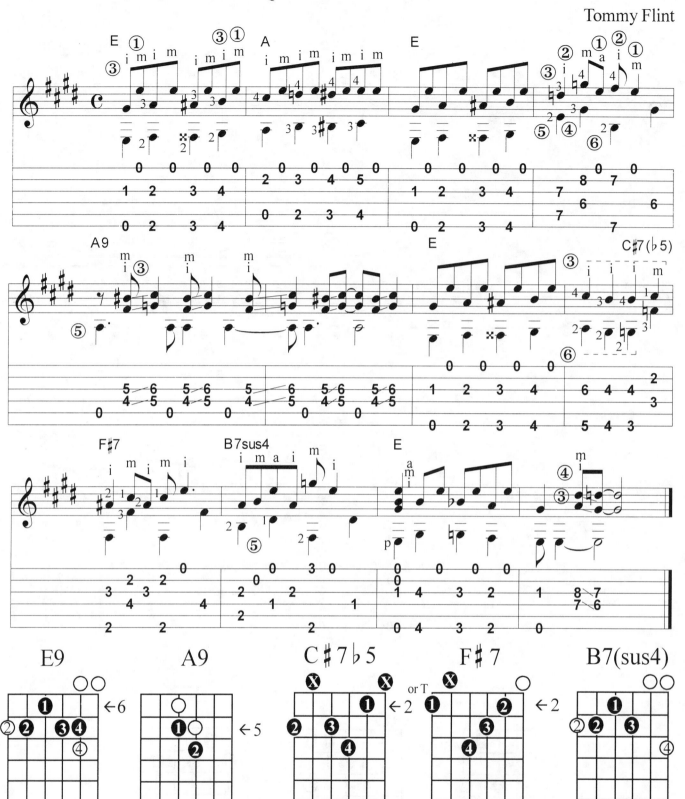

LEGEND OF THE CARPATHIANS

Moderate

Tommy Flint

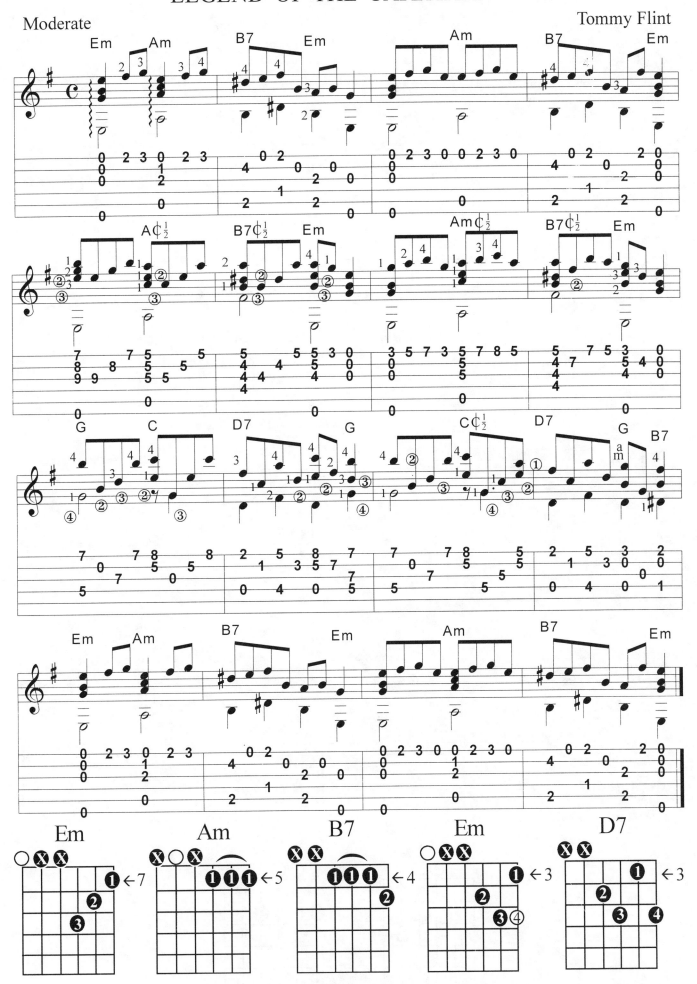

THE CARNIVAL OF VENICE

SLURS
THE UPWARD SLUR OR HAMMER ON

The upward slur or hammer on will be indicated by a curved line. To hammer on, pluck an open string and while the string is still ringing hammer (press down abruptly) the left hand finger on the correct note. It is also possible to hold a string down at any fret and using a different left hand finger hammer the string on a higher fret. Pick the first note. Do not pick the second note.

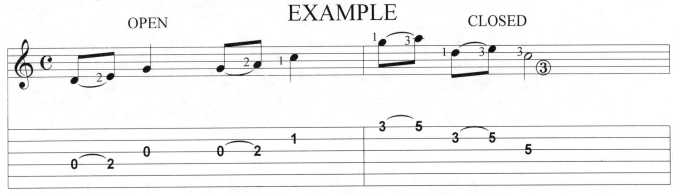

THE DOWNWARD SLUR OR PULL OFF

The downward slur or pull off is the opposite of hammering on. Strike the higher note. Then while it is still ringing pull the finger off, thus allowing the lower note to sound. Do not just lift the finger, but pull off at an angle (to the side). Actually the finger plucks the string as it is pulled off.

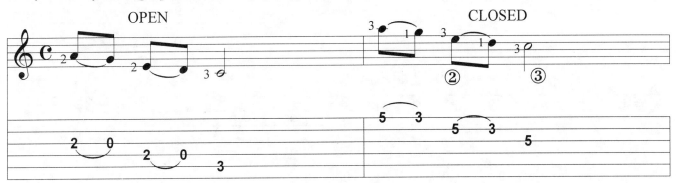

THE SLIDE

To slide into a note or chord place the fingers one or more frets below the note you intend to play. Immediately, after striking the note or chord slide up to the correct position, while keeping the fingers depressed on the strings. Pick the first note. Do not pick the second note, slide into it.

In the first example, pick the C notes on the "and" after the count of four. Slide into the C♯ note on the count of one.

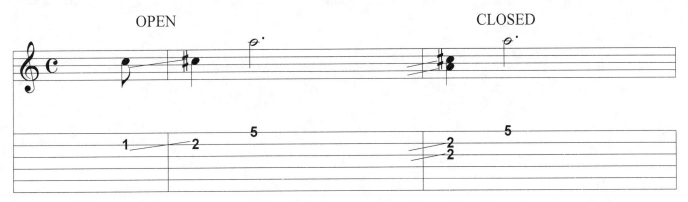

WILDWOOD FLOWER

HOW TO PLAY IN ANY KEY

Let us review the "blues progression." It is twelve measures, or twelve bars in length. The basic blues is in most cases, four bars of the tonic or I chord, two bars of the sub-dominant or IV chord, two more bars of the I chord, one bar of the dominant or V chord, one bar of IV and two more bars of I

Example:

I	I	I	I
IV	IV	I	I
V	IV	I	I.

The location of the I, IV and V form a triangle.   **TRIANGLE**

WALKING BLUES
KEY OF G

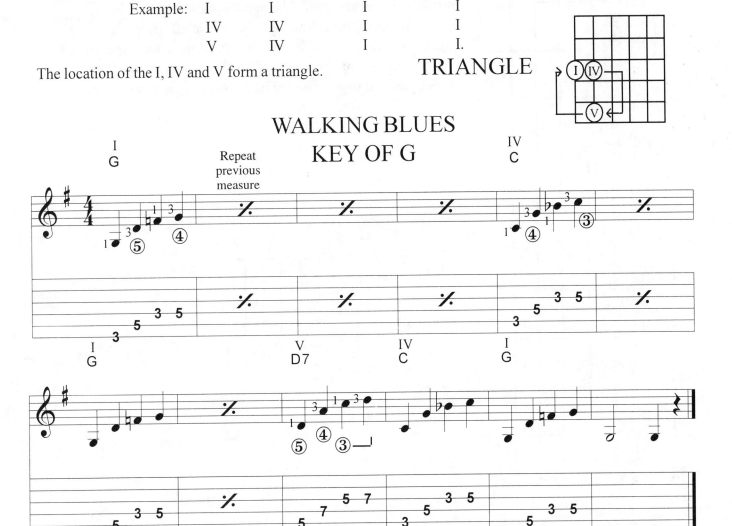

On the next page is a chart of the letter names of the notes on the ⑥ and ⑤ strings. The solo you just played was in the key of G. I, was on the ⑥ string and IV and V were on the ⑤ string. To play the same solo in the key of A, just move every note two frets higher. Then, I and IV are on the fifth fret and V is on the seventh fret. Or, in the key of C, I and IV are on the eighth fret and V is on the tenth.

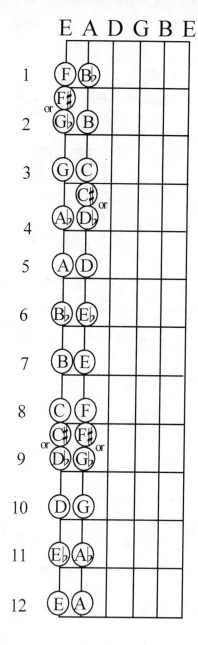

E A D G B E

It would be very difficult to play this solo (using the same triangle) higher than the ninth or tenth fret on a guitar that is not cutaway. So, to play it in the key of D, Eb or E we just need to use a differently shaped triangle and start on the ⑤th string. For instance, in the key of D, I is on the ⑤th string, fifth fret; IV is on the ⑥ string, third fret; and V is on the ⑥ string, fifth fret. Also, using this triangle keeps the notes lower that might sound too high in the upper positions. This is good for some things such as boogies and rhythm on the bass strings, power chords, etc.

TRIANGLE

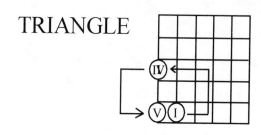

WALKING BLUES
KEY OF D

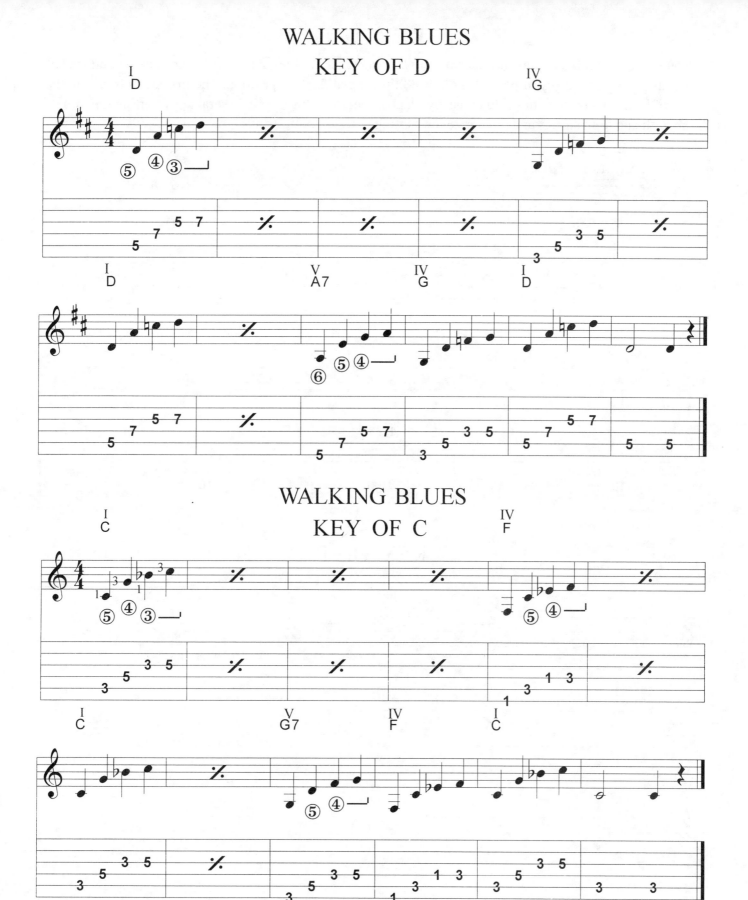

WALKING BLUES
KEY OF C

KEY OF F

You see it is possible to play the same pattern starting on either the ⑥ or ⑤th string. The second study on this page is in the key of F starting on the ⑥th string at the first position. The first study is also in the key of F starting on the 5th string at the eighth position. Play this solo in several keys starting on both the ⑥th and ⑤th strings and memorize the starting notes on both strings.

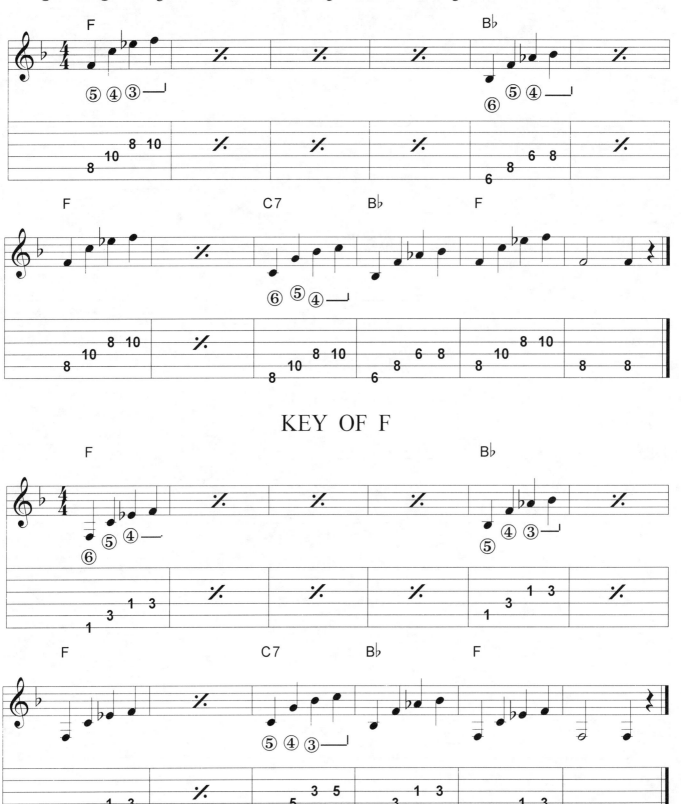

KEY OF F

74

STOMPING ON THE STEPPE

Tommy Flint

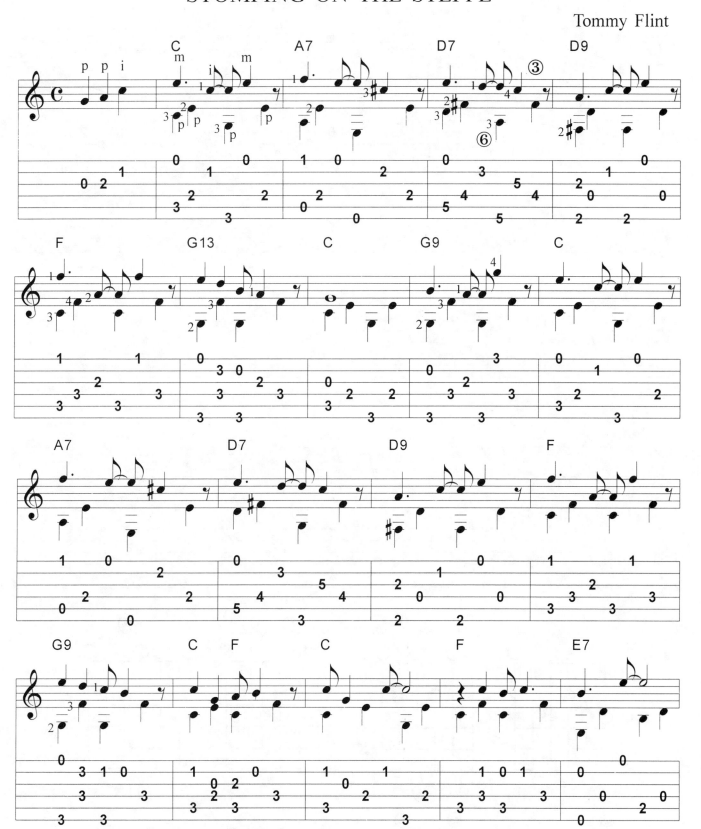

SATISFACTION GUARANTEED

Tommy Flint

ETUDE

Moderato   Hold chords   Tommy Flint

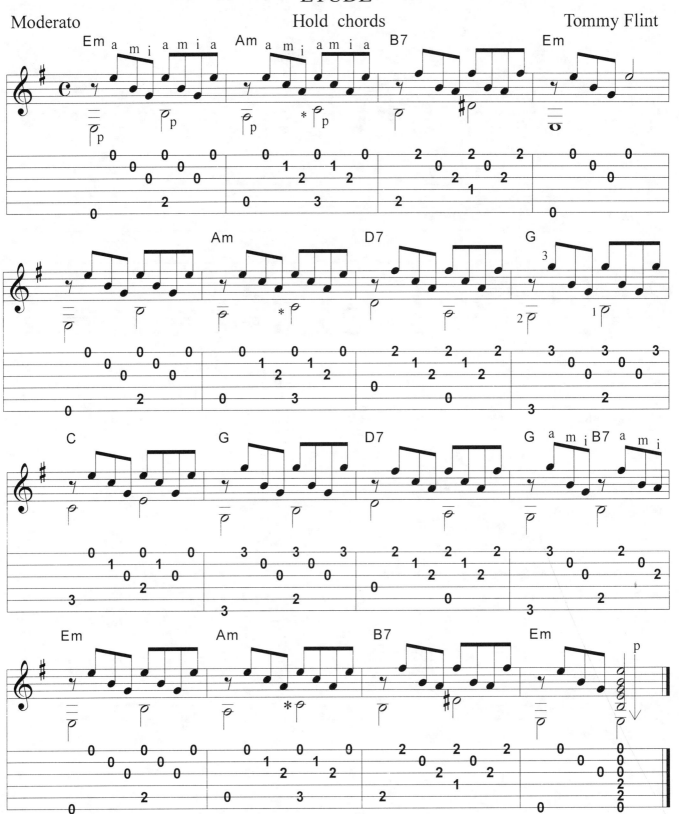

* If it is too difficult to play C note while holding Am chord, E note on the ④ string may be substituted.

When changing from D7 to G chord the fingering shown at right is preferred. When changing from C to G use original fingering.

G

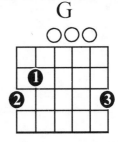

TWO NEW CHORDS   AMAZING GRACE

G7   G13

When playing in 3/4 or waltz time, the thumb and index finger are frequently used together to play the rhythm strokes. In measure number one of the following solo, the thumb and middle finger are used on the first beat. The thumb and index finger are used to play the rhythm stroke on the second beat. The middle and index fingers are used for the eighth notes on the third beat.

rit = Gradually decrease tempo. Slow down.   ⌢• = Fermata. This sign indicates a long pause. Hold the note. Sustain.

THE CAPO

The capo is a device that may be clamped on the neck of the guitar to shorten the length of the "open" strings. It can be placed on any fret directly behind the fret wire.

There are various kinds of capos. One type is held in place by an elastic band, another is clamped in position by a spring and there is the screw type. I prefer a capo that clips on the neck and can easily be moved with one hand.

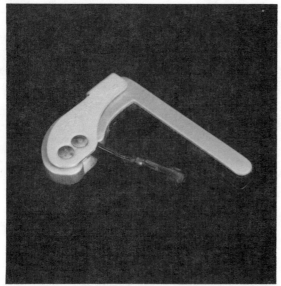

CAPO THAT I USE

ELASTIC CAPO

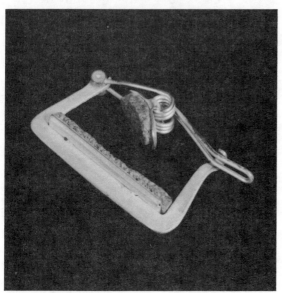

CAPO MERLE TRAVIS USED

HOW CAPO FITS ON NECK

HOW TO USE THE CAPO

Remember, there are only seven natural notes, or letter names in the musical alphabet. The distance between any two natural notes is a whole step (or two frets) except B to C and E to F, which are half steps. However, between the natural notes are the sharps and flats, so the half steps also have names. Actually, there are twelve tones when we include the sharps and flats.

As you know, the sharp raises a note a half step and a flat lowers it a half step. For instance, the ① string, first fret is F. When we raise it to the second fret it becomes F♯. The first string, third fret is G. When we lower it to the second fret it becomes G♭. So you see some notes have more than one name. F♯ and G♭ are at the same location on the fingerboard (the same fret and string).

THE TWELVE TONES

A	A♯	B	C	C♯	D	D♯	E	F	F♯	G	G♯
	B♭			D♭		E♭			G♭		A♭

On the next page is a chart of chords and what the names of the chords become when the capo is used. As an example, when the capo is on the first fret, C becomes C♯ or D♭ or, if the capo is placed on the fifth fret, the chord becomes F. This holds true for all types of chords, whether it is major, minor, seventh, etc.

The capo is a valuable tool for the guitarist who likes the open-string sound and for the beginner who has not yet learned movable chords. Maybe you have learned a song in the key of C, but that key is just too low for your voice. By experimenting with placing the capo on different frets and using the same chord forms, or fingering, it is possible to find the key best suited to your voice. If the capo is on the third fret you are in the key of E♭, or if it is on the sixth fret you are in F♯ or G♭.

But this is not the only reason the capo is used. Some great guitarists use it because it creates a bright ringing tone. Merle Travis sometimes used a capo because he liked the tone of his guitar when he used it. I have also seen Chat Atkins, Thom Bresh and Buster B. Jones use capos. Buster sometimes uses two or more capos, by capoing the ⑥ and ⑤ strings at one position and the ①, ②, ③ and ④ strings at a different position.

CAPO CHART

CHORD HELD

When Capo on Fret #	C	G	D	A	E	B	F or	A#/Bb	D#/Eb or	G#/Ab	C#/Db	F#/Gb
1	C#/Db	G#/Ab	D#/Eb	A#/Bb	F	C	F#/Gb	B	E	A	D	G
2	D	A	E	B	F#/Gb	C#/Db	G	C	F	A#/Bb	D#/Eb	G#/Ab
3	D#/Eb	A#/Bb	F	C	G	D	G#/Ab	C#/Db	F#/Gb	B	E	A
4	E	B	F#/Gb	C#/Db	G#/Ab	D#/Eb	A	D	G	C	F	A#/Bb
5	F	C	G	D	A	E	A#/Bb	D#/Eb	G#/Ab	C#/Db	F#/Gb	B
6	F#/Gb	C#/Db	G#/Ab	D#/Eb	A#/Bb	F	B	E	A	D	G	C
7	G	D	A	E	B	F#/Gb	C	F	A#/Bb	D#/Eb	G#/Ab	C#/Db
8	G#/Ab	D#/Eb	A#/Bb	F	C	G	C#/Db	F#/Gb	B	E	A	D
9	A	E	B	F#/Gb	C#/Db	G#/Ab	D	G	C	F	A#/Bb	D#/Eb
10	A#/Bb	F	C	G	D	A	D#/Eb	G#/Ab	C#/Db	F#/Gb	B	E
11	B	F#/Gb	C#/Db	G#/Ab	D#/Eb	A#/Bb	E	A	D	G	C	F
12	C	G	D	A	E	B	F	A#/Bb	D#/Eb	G#/Ab	C#/Db	F#/Gb

BECOMES

As you know, the I, IV and V chords in the key of C are C-F-G7. When you place the capo on the first fret, the same chord forms become C#-F#-G#7 (or they could be Db-Gb-Ab7), or when the capo is on the third fret the chords become Eb-Ab-Bb7. At this time play some of the tunes you have learned, using the capo in various positions. When you have determined the key you are in, speak the name of the key or write it. This will help you remember where to place the capo for a particular key.

THE BALLAD OF JESSE JAMES

Russellville, in southwest Kentucky, is one of the most beautiful towns I have visited. It has some wonderful historic buildings and antebellum homes. One of those buildings, which is now a museum, was a bank a century ago. There is a bullet hole in the door that Jesse James put there as he was riding away after robbing that bank. This melody reminds me of that.

83

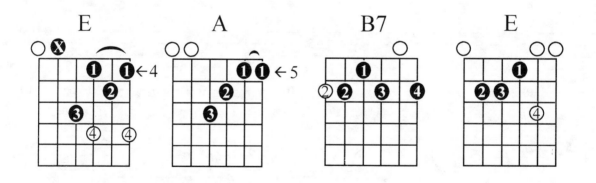

COCKLES AND MUSSELS

SOME VERY USEFUL PATTERNS

The following patterns may be used as accompaniment to songs. They are also great technique builders.
Play each pattern in a slow relaxed manner, then, gradually increase the tempo each day, or each playing
session. You will be surprised how easy these patterns will seem in a few days.

No. 1

Play the melody of Aura Lee until you feel comfortable with it, then, while singing or humming the melody, play the accompaniment using one or more of the patterns you learned on the previous page. You might use pattern numbers three through the first eight bars and number four through the last eight.

AURA LEE

MOVABLE CHORDS

The following chords can be played in any position on the fingerboard. However, each chord will have a different name on each fret. When the three chords are played on the same fret they are the principal, or I, IV and V chords of a major key which has the same name as the first chord. For instance, at the first fret, the key of F, or in the sixth position, the key of B♭.

I have shown two forms (fingerings) of each chord on the first four strings and the four inside strings.

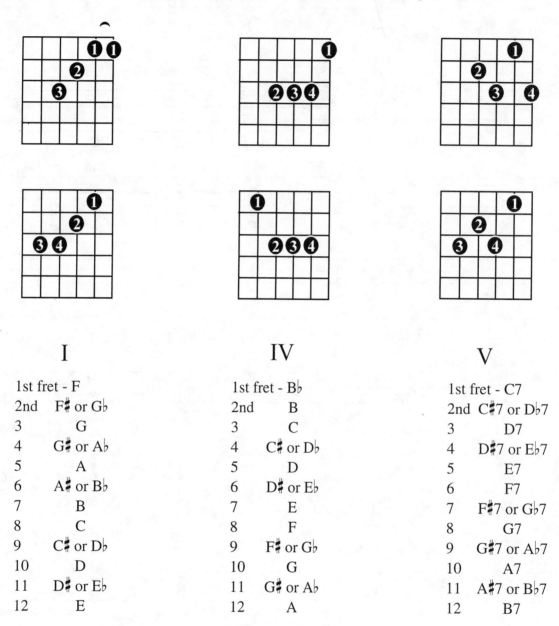

I		IV		V	
1st fret -	F	1st fret -	B♭	1st fret -	C7
2nd	F♯ or G♭	2nd	B	2nd	C♯7 or D♭7
3	G	3	C	3	D7
4	G♯ or A♭	4	C♯ or D♭	4	D♯7 or E♭7
5	A	5	D	5	E7
6	A♯ or B♭	6	D♯ or E♭	6	F7
7	B	7	E	7	F♯7 or G♭7
8	C	8	F	8	G7
9	C♯ or D♭	9	F♯ or G♭	9	G♯7 or A♭7
10	D	10	G	10	A7
11	D♯ or E♭	11	G♯ or A♭	11	A♯7 or B♭7
12	E	12	A	12	B7

Remember, when you reach the twelfth fret you are starting over on a short scale fingerboard. The thirteenth fret has the same name as the first.

Notice that opens strings can be used with the A, D and E7 movable chords.

THE ROLLING FLINT HILLS

Tommy Flint

The following solo makes use of several of the chord forms shown on page 86. Watch for the position markings. Notice that the open ①st string is used with B♭ chord in the second measure. In the second measure of the second ending you will use a five-string F chord. Form the chord on the four inside strings, then straighten the first finger to lie flat on the ①st string. You will also find some syncopation in this arrangement.

ONCE UPON A TIME

Tommy Flint

THE NASHVILLE NUMBER SYSTEM

SOMETIMES CALLED NASHVILLE SHORTHAND

The Nashville Number System is used in Nashville by session players in recording studios, awards shows, some live performances and by the Grand Ole Opry staff band. It is an extremely fast and easy method of communicating chord progressions and arrangements and is very easy to transpose.

The number system is based on the major, and sometimes the minor scale. As you know from reading about the scale on page 60, there are eighth notes in the scale, the eighth being the same as the first, only an octave higher. The degrees of the scale are numbered:

1	2	3	4	5	6	7	8
C	D	E	F	G	A	B	C

Since the eighth note has the same name as the first, we can eliminate the eighth. We will use only the numbers 1 through 7.

Remember the blues progression you studied earlier in this book? It uses only the one, four and five chords and is a twelve bar progression. In Nashville we use Arabic numerals because it seems they can be written much faster and easier than other styles. So, the blues progression looks like this:

$$\begin{array}{ccccc} C & 1 & 1 & 1 & 1 \\ & 4 & 4 & 1 & 1 \\ & 5 & 5 & 1 & 1 \end{array}$$

The letter C written at the beginning tells you the key. If the man singing this song in the key of C has a female singing partner her voice might be up a fourth. So, we could modulate to F for the second chorus. Just place a small number seven behind the last "one" in the twelfth measure. That will tell you to play a seventh chord which will cause the modulation to sound very smooth and natural. The two choruses would look like this.

$$\frac{4}{4} \quad \begin{array}{ccccc} C & 1 & 1 & 1 & 1 \\ & 4 & 4 & 1 & 1 \\ & 5 & 5 & 1 & 1^7 \end{array}$$

$$\begin{array}{ccccc} F & 1 & 1 & 1 & 1 \\ & 4 & 4 & 1 & 1 \\ & 5 & 5 & 1 & 1 \end{array}$$

Notice the time signature before the key. When you modulated up a fourth the "one" chord became F, so find the key of F on the chart on the next page. The fourth is B♭ and the fifth is C.

The following chart shows you the notes in all major scales

KEY	SCALE					
1	2	3	4	5	6	7
C	D	E	F	G	A	B
G	A	B	C	D	E	F♯
D	E	F♯	G	A	B	C♯
A	B	C♯	D	E	F♯	G♯
E	F♯	G♯	A	B	C♯	D♯
B	C♯	D♯	E	F♯	G♯	A♯
F♯	G♯	A♯	B	C♯	D♯	E♯
C♯	D♯	E♯	F♯	G♯	A♯	B♯
F	G	A	B♭	C	D	E
B♭	C	D	E♭	F	G	A
E♭	F	G	A♭	B♭	C	D
A♭	B♭	C	D♭	E♭	F	G
D♭	E♭	F	G♭	A♭	B♭	C
G♭	A♭	B♭	C♭	D♭	E♭	F
C♭	D♭	E♭	F♭	G♭	A♭	B♭

All numbers will be considered major chords unless some type of sign shows it to be a different type. The minor chord will be indicated by a minus sign (-). Example: 2- The augmented fifth will be indicated by a plus sign (+). Example: 1+

A small "o" after a number tells you the chord is diminished, or dim 7. The dominant seventh chord will be written as a small 7 behind the primary number. Example: 5^7. In fact, all type chords will be written in the same manner, 4^9, 1^{11}, 5^{13}, 2-^7. The major seventh will be shown by a triangle after the number. Example: $1^{\triangle}$

Altered chords will be shown by small numbers and a ♯ or ♭ sign after the primary number. Examples: $5^{7\flat5}$, $1^{13\flat9}$.

Sometimes a bass note is under the primary number. Example: $\dfrac{1}{3}$ $\dfrac{1}{5}$ $\dfrac{1}{5\sharp}$

Usually, when the musicians have set up and are in tune, the producer or engineer plays the demo tape and the musicians write the numbers as they listen. If it would happen to be a song using the melody of the old tune "I'm Thinking Tonight of My Blue Eyes," the leader might ask, "Do we all have the same thing? Here it is: Eleven, forty-four, fifty-five, eleven, eleven, forty-four, fifty-five, eleven. Let's run through it once." Then he might say, "Let's use this for the intro: sixteen, twenty-two, fifty-five, one, four over five. Use seventh chords on everything in the intro except the ones and the four over five." It would look like this:

$$
\begin{array}{c c c c}
\text{Intro} & 1 & 6^7 & 2^7 & 2^7 \\
& 5^7 & 5^7 & 1 & \dfrac{4}{5}
\end{array}
$$

$$
\begin{array}{c c c c}
1 & 1 & 4 & 4 \\
5 & 5 & 1 & 1 \\
1 & 1 & 4 & 4 \\
5 & 5 & 1 & 1
\end{array}
$$

If there are two pick-up notes they will be shown by small marks (" or ♩♩). When there is more than one chord in a measure it is called a split measure and will be written with a diagonal line separating the chords (1/6 2/5). Some people draw a box around the split measure:

$\boxed{1/6}$ $\boxed{2/5}$

The little marks above the numbers indicate the number of beats on each chord.

" "   " "
1/6   2/5.

Example of how an intro might look.

$$4/3\text{-} \quad 2\text{-}/6^7 \quad 2\text{-}^7/5^7 \quad 1/5^7+$$

What famous standard would this intro fit?

SOME PERFORMANCE TIPS

ATTITUDE

I believe that a positive attitude is the most important quality the guitarist can possess. It is definitely an asset. When you walk on stage worried about playing a difficult passage, afraid you might make a mistake, you will most likely fumble when you get to that point. Instead, play and play and be prepared and when you walk on stage say to yourself, "I feel confident. I am prepared and I will do my best. I expect to give a good performance." If you feel that way it will likely happen. Remember, in most cases, expectancy determines outcome.

Also, friendliness and cooperation are very helpful. Although, some sour natured, arrogant musicians have succeeded in spite of themselves, that is not usually the case.

ON BACKING OTHERS

When you are the featured performer always perform to the best of your ability. Shine, show what you can do, bring the audience to its feet. But, when backing another musician or vocalist, it is very important that you remember to help that featured performer who is out in front to sound as good as possible. You don't need to show off all your hot licks while backing up a vocalist.

A mature musician knows that when not to play is just as important as when to play. He/she knows how to accompany other musicians or vocalists without covering them up. Performing with another musician is actually having conversation with another person. We say what we have to say, express our thoughts or feelings; then we listen, and allow others to hear what our musical partner has to say. That is why we don't show off our hot licks and fast, fancy fingerwork while the vocalist is at the microphone, or an instrumentalist is taking a chorus.

When you are out in front doing your "stuff" you need to expect the support and backing of your accompanists, and they need to be considerate enough to not butt in or cover you up.

I worked with bands for many years of my life and still occasionally play a gig with a band, although most dates now are for solo performances and workshops. In any case, I have played for many, many people who were not guitarists, or even musicians, but who loved music, loved to dance, etc. So, music must sometimes be entertaining not just technical. In order to be a successful musician, it is sometimes necessary to play for others, not just ourselves to be successful, etc.

THE IMPORTANCE
OF PLAYING MUSIC WITH OTHERS

Now that you can play the melody as well as accompaniment of some songs, I believe it would be beneficial for you to occasionally play with other musicians, preferably another guitarist. You might play the melody while the other person plays accompaniment or, if he/she can sing or play some melodies, you can play rhythm, or try filling in the open spaces between the lines or phrases of words or music.

Playing music with others, keeping time, switching parts (melody, rhythm, etc.) are very helpful in learning when to play forcefully and with authority, or when to play softer and assist the other musician. Be alert, listen, watch, anticipate the next move, be aware of what is happening.

There are some great solo guitarists who possess incredible technique and can perform complex arrangements, but have great difficulty working with others. They are virtually helpless when called on to play a harmony line with another instrument, to comp and back up a vocalist, to trade fours, or improvise a chorus.

I believe that the ability to perform in most any setting is very important and an attribute of the real guitarist. Then when you become a great soloist, you will have some valuable experience and knowledge.

GENOA HOLIDAY

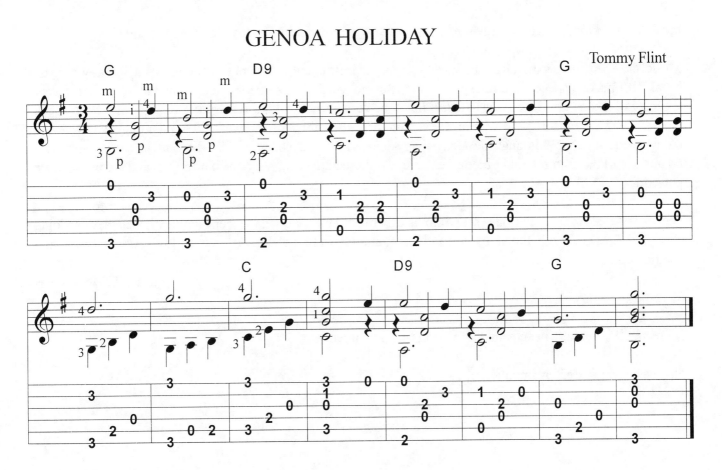

Tommy Flint

MORE ABOUT TABLATURE

Tablature is not a replacement for standard music notation. Although, it is a fast and easy method to use to learn to play the guitar and a very fast way of writing and reading melodies and chords, it is only an aid.

If you are satisfied with playing tab that was written specifically for the guitar or to play chords to accompany a vocalist, tab will suffice. Since guitar tab is written specifically for guitar, you will not be able to read tab written for other instruments (banjo, mandolin, etc.) and play it on your guitar. If you want to learn a new solo, you will have to ask or hire a more experienced guitarist to write the tab for you, at least until your ear has developed enough that you can hear the chord changes and learn to play the melody by ear. You will not be able to learn songs from sheet music or song books that are in most cases written for piano and vocal.

If you plan on, at some point, being a competent guitarist I would suggest that you learn to read music and study theory, harmony, etc. Learn how to build chords, transpose, be able to play any song in any key. Be able to work in any setting from playing in bands to solo concerts, recording sessions, live shows, movie sound tracks or whatever you need to do. I recommend my book and recording: "DE-LUXE FINGERSTYLE GUITAR METHOD" vol. 1, Mel Bay Publications, #4 Industrial Drive, Pacific, MO 63069-0066.

ORIGINALITY

I feel that, for a musician to be truly great, he or she has to be different. At least, different in some way.

Music, like speech is communication. When you play an instrument your personality comes out, just as when you speak. If I make a speech and repeat exactly the same words that someone before me has spoken, then my speech will mean very little to the listener. It will be very uninteresting. We need to describe and express our thoughts and feelings in our own words, even on the same subject. And we need to play our own ideas and thoughts on our guitar. Although, the Gettysburg Address is a great piece of work, when I recite those words, they do not impart the emotion that Lincoln felt. He was there at the cemetery, the battlefield, and his words were powerful.

I believe we need to study the masters and emulate them until we have some understanding of what they are doing or saying. We need to listen and study and learn, and begin to develop our own style so we can create and communicate.

Your music needs your personality!

Mona Lisa has already been painted. We don't need another.

No one becomes great by imitation.